SIMPSONISTAS

Tales from the Simpson Family Literary Project

Vol. 1

SIMPSONISTAS

Tales from the Simpson Family Literary Project

Vol. 1

Storytelling is the foundation of a literate society.

Joseph Di Prisco, Editor

This is a Genuine Vireo Book

A Vireo Book | Rare Bird Books
453 South Spring Street, Suite 302
Los Angeles, CA 90013
rarebirdbooks.com

First Trade Paperback Original Edition

Set in Dante
Printed in the United States

10 9 8 7 6 5 4 3 2 1

CIP data available on request

Dedicated to Sharon Simpson
& In honor of the memory of Barclay Simpson

CONTENTS

9   **Joseph Di Prisco**, The Simpson Family Literary Project: An Introduction

22 *Acknowledgments*

24 *Permissions*

25 **Anthony Marra**, "The Last Words of Benito Picone," a story

35 **T. Geronimo Johnson**, *Welcome to Braggsville*, excerpt from the novel

41 **T. Geronimo Johnson**, UC Berkeley English Department Commencement Address 2017

53 **Lori Ostlund**, "Clear as Cake," a story

71 **Ben Fountain**, "Impasse Tempête," a story

75 **Joyce Carol Oates**, "'A Wounded Deer—Leaps Highest': Motives for Metaphor," an essay

87 **Joyce Carol Oates**, *Hazards of Time Travel,* excerpt from the novel

95 *How Stories Make the World*: Bay Area Book Festival Panel Discussion: Anthony Marra, Ismail Muhammad, Joyce Carol Oates, Scott Saul; Joseph Di Prisco, moderator

127 **Samantha Hunt**, "Cortés the Killer," a story

141 **Martin Pousson**, "Revival Girl," a story

151 **Geoffrey O'Brien**, Poems

SIMPSON PROJECT FELLOWS
AND WORKSHOP STUDENTS

163 **Contra Costa County Juvenile Detention**; Mt. McKinley High School, Martinez, California; Contra Costa County Library

165 **Ismail Muhammad**, "An Unbearable Tension: On James Baldwin and the Nation of Islam," an essay

Authors identified by initials

174 **J. P.**, *Untitled*

175 **I. O.**, *Untitled*

176 **S. R.**, *Phoenix*

Northgate High School; Walnut Creek, California

177 **Lise Gaston**, "Cityscapes in Mating Season," a poem

185 **Eliana Goldstein**, "Sunset in Mexico"; "Winter"

189 **Grace Decker**, "Calef Avenue"

190 **Logan Vendel**, "A Lazy Midsummer Brunch"; "Traveling"

193 **Jackson Mills**, "Refugee"

194 **Livia Doporto**, "Not my Mama"; "Just a Smile"

Girls Inc., Alameda County; Oakland, California

197 **Laura Ritland**, Poems

202 **Tiffany Tong**, "It Starts with You"

203 **Kerry Lin**, "Half of a Heart"

204 **Michaela Dunaway**, "The Darkness"; "Defense: A Memoir"

207 *Contributors*

THE SIMPSON FAMILY LITERARY PROJECT
AN INTRODUCTION

BY JOSEPH DI PRISCO

What would our lives be like without storytelling?

That's not a rhetorical question. Without stories, our lives would be, quite literally, unimaginable.

Storytelling may not be *everything*, but sometimes when you catch yourself being swept up in a story, transported by the narrative, it can feel in the moment close to being everything, whatever everything might provisionally stand for besides everything. Crazy overstated? Maybe. Nevertheless, that is something like the case that T. Geronimo Johnson, 2017 Simpson Prize Recipient, makes about the importance of stories in his supercharged and allusive Berkeley commencement address, found here in these pages. To quote Johnson, "Humans cannot survive without story any more than they can survive without sunlight."

Consider also Joyce Carol Oates, Simpson Project Writer-in-Residence. She fashions a tantalizing, related argument in her illuminating, wide-ranging essay, "'A Wounded Deer—Leaps Highest': Motives for Metaphor," included here as well, about writers artfully, urgently "bearing witness" in their stories, novels, and poems. In Oates's words, "'Bearing witness' means giving voice to those whose voices have been muted, or destroyed; those who have been victims; those whose stories require a larger audience than they have received."

Insights such as these resonate intensely for the Simpson Family Literary Project. Storytelling fosters empathy. Stories elicit passions and refine reflections. They bind us together in the language, and languages, of our shared humanity. It may seem distressingly self-evident that meaningful connections between people can sometimes prove elusive in our radically contentious Twitter / Facebook / Instagram / AI epoch. As far as the Simpson Project is concerned, however, it's worth each ounce of energy, each investment of imagination, expended in the efforts to forge such life-affirming linkages—in and through stories. We believe that storytelling, when it kicks in, when it is internalized, when it is taught, creates and enriches communities. And if we frame storytelling that way, perhaps we just might be oonching closer and closer to the nongentrified, unboundaried worldwide neighborhood where, well, everything might indeed *be* very much on the table.

MISSION

The Simpson Project promotes literacy and literature, writers and writing across generations.

As a matter both of principle and practice, the Project sponsors creative writing and reading inside and outside schools, libraries, colleges, and universities. Across an expansive social and educational and literary spectrum, we champion new literature and authors of all ages. We strive to enhance the daily lives of readers and writers of all generations: educators, librarians, students, and authors in diverse communities throughout California and the country. We do so not only because we intrinsically value literature and the art of the story, but also because we are committed to this bracing, underpinning proposition: *Storytelling is the foundation of a literate society.*

As articulated, that proposition virtually functions as our mantra. It holds the key to "reading" as well as "writing" the Simpson Project. As we all would acknowledge, literacy for both children and adults is an indispensable necessity not merely to survive but to ultimately thrive. Literacy pumps life through the heart of a society that should aspire to be humane, democratic, and equitable. That is why we are universally obliged to intentionally cultivate, widely and deeply, literacy and literacies—not only language literacy, but civic, scientific, artistic, technological, media, mathematical, financial, medical, ecological, and all the other related literacies required to navigate the shoals and the depths of contemporary realities. Unleashing the power of these literacies fundamentally depends upon faculties developed through critical thinking as well as, we believe, creative reading and writing.

As commonly conceived, however, notions of literacy and literature have been typically compartmentalized. The Simpson Project instead removes that barrier—and couples the two. Brain research and common sense both underscore how complex is the attainment of literacy. Ultimately, literacy goes beyond grasping the mechanics of reading and writing. It may seem rational that a command of mechanics and syntax is a precondition for creative writing. But that is not quite so. The drive to exercise reading and writing skills merges seamlessly with the desire to create. As experienced teachers testify, students with the desire to speak their minds and hearts, to bring to life on the page the figures of their imagination, come to master the mechanics. And with reassurance, practice, conversation, and instruction, they are able to express themselves with nuance, purpose, freedom, and authority—in other words, in art, story, memoir, poetry.

Stories also bind families together over generations. Shared stories build community, and awareness of shared experience, values, and aspirations creates culture. All told, individual and communal contributions to storytelling illuminate the essential humanity binding us all. Stories enable us to recognize and respect the wide range of differing assumptions, beliefs and perspectives that inform our daily lives.

We believe, therefore, that the advancing of literacy intertwines with the crafting of stories, with reading and writing literature. After all, storytelling is how we read ourselves and others in an increasingly complex world, how we come to terms with our existence, searching out its meaning and purpose. Literature makes us literate, that is, even as literacy ushers in literature.

Already I'm sensing caution signs possibly looming. So let's beware of boulders in the path. I don't ever wish to imply that stories are way too serious to be enjoyed. Were that the case, probably our most cherished stories, the ones that thrilled and exalted and pleased and taught us, would never have been composed, and, from our vantage point, the Simpson Project would have never been conceived.

THE PROJECT

The Project traces its origins back not so long ago, to Summer 2015. That's when we were, and will always continue to be, moved to action by the breathtaking philanthropic example of Sharon and the late

Barclay Simpson, who was a legendary titan of industry. Their altruistic leadership and generosity—with the University of California, Berkeley; The Berkeley Art Museum / Pacific Film Archive; California College of the Arts; Girls Inc.; The California Shakespeare Theater; The Lafayette Public Library, and countless other causes and institutions serving children, education, and the arts—makes for a spine-tingling, dazzling story of optimism in its own right. As larger-than-life Barc paraphrased Martin Luther King Jr., "Don't forget that the only thing that makes philanthropy necessary is social injustice."

Since its beginning, the Simpson Project has conceived and administered:

1) Simpson Project Writing Workshops for younger writers led by Simpson Fellows from the University of California, Berkeley, English Department (in 2018) at a boy-identified unit of a juvenile hall, at an afterschool program for underserved urban girls, and at a comprehensive and diverse public high school;

2) the annual $50,000 Simpson Literary Prize for an author of fiction in the middle of a burgeoning career, who is in residence for part of the spring in Berkeley and in Lafayette, conferring with students, faculty, and librarians;

3) the Writer-in-Residence at the Lafayette Public Library in partnership with the Lafayette Library and Learning Center, a towering literary presence who contributes to the lives of students and librarians and the community at large;

And 4) this anthology of creative work, *Simpsonistas*, by Simpson Project–related artists, ranging from a world-famous, iconic author and working writers of distinction—to, for instance, incarcerated high school-age young men and high school-age young women aspiring to be first-generation college students, all of whom appear for the first time in print.

In order for us to exist, we rely upon institutional authorization and commitment. So it is that the nonprofit Simpson Family Literary Project is the product of the unique, multi-tendril, private/public collaboration of the Lafayette Library and Learning Center Foundation (LLLCF), of Lafayette, California, and the University of California, Berkeley, English Department, and we gratefully operate under the 501(c)3 aegis of the LLLCF. The LLLCF and the Berkeley English Department, who are both committed to community outreach, underwrite significant pass-through costs of education and administration through in-kind contributions, while the bulk of the cash moneys come from generous donors, expenditures and fundraising overseen and managed by the Simpson Project Committee. Committee members from these two leading institutions collaborate and play vital roles in this separate and distinct initiative known as the Simpson Project: visionaries and trailblazers from the Contra Costa County communities in tandem with distinguished and dedicated Berkeley professors and authors. If you have ever been professionally associated with a philanthropically sustained non-profit or an educational enterprise or any multifaceted, complex organization, for that matter, you appreciate how wonderful, and rare, is the spirit of collegiality. The camaraderie that we enjoy in the Project is something never to be taken for granted.

The inaugural publication of the Project, *Simpsonistas: Vol. 1—Tales from the Simpson Family Literary Project*, gathers selected work by several Simpson Literary Prize Finalists of 2017 and 2018; Joyce Carol Oates (Simpson Project Writer-in-Residence at the Lafayette Public Library: Winter/Spring 2018 and 2019); Simpson Project Committee members; Simpson Fellows (graduate student, professionally accomplished writers and teachers selected from the English Department of the University of California, Berkeley); and fledgling high school-age writers in Simpson Writing Workshops (conducted Winter/Spring 2018 at Contra Costa County, California, Juvenile Hall; Girls Inc., Alameda County, California; and Northgate High School, Walnut Creek, California). This is the first volume in the projected periodic series of *Simpsonistas*.

THE SIMPSON LITERARY PRIZE

We award the annual prize, not for a single major work, but to an outstanding, significant author. Specifically, the Prize goes to a distinguished mid-career American writer, whom we define as one who has published a minimum of two sterling, well-regarded works of fiction, novels or books of short stories, composed in English, though some Finalists enjoy more extensive publishing résumés. The monetary award, $50,000, is intended to be substantial enough to maximize impact. Eligibility has no restriction as to author's age or geography, subject matter or style. In fact, our 2017 and 2018 finalists come from across the country, and range in age from the thirties to the fifties; their books run the gamut of narrative structures and styles, and are rooted in various literary traditions. They are published by prestigious houses, either those of venerable standing or upcoming independents, large, small, nonprofit, and commercial, coast to coast. A jury winnows down the nominated authors to a shortlist of finalists, from which the recipient is selected. The only other limitation is that this is a writer who has yet to receive capstone recognition, such as a Pulitzer, a National Book Award, or a MacArthur, though we might be forgiven for expecting it is likely just a matter of time till that oversight is remedied.

Why *mid-career*?

If you travel in or near publishing and literary circles you are familiar with the term "emerging writers." Its meaning seems plainly self-evident. Emerging writers are gifted, younger writers just finding their voice, beginning to publish and gain a reputation. Every year, a number of highly covetable awards and fellowships go to these impressive artists. Publishers clamor and compete to publish them, banking on hopes that one of them someday becomes the Next Big Thing or writes The Next Great Book. That's the way the market works, and there's nothing surprising or anything but benign about it. But upon reflection, there is something curious about the term.

Unlike with the case of butterflies who emerge marvelous from their cocoon ordeals, the emergence of writers is more complicated still. Some geniuses do indeed spectacularly arrive one day on the scene, while others develop slowly, over time, often maddeningly and even perhaps erratically for authors and their fans. The arc of a writer's career can be long and it bends to—who would dare predict?

It's obviously fortunate for younger, emerging writers to feel the love and recognition, not to mention to enjoy the influx of real dollars. But writers at all stages feel that selfsame need. The fact is, there are precious few major prizes on the order of the Simpson Prize catering to mid-career writers. It's worth noting, too, that at the midpoint of writers' careers it's often a challenge to publish or grow an audience. Only a tiny percentage of them will ever ascend the best-seller lists, or be able to care for themselves and their families on the proceeds, and effectively none will sell units like a Stephen King or a J. K. Rowling. Now that they have arrived at this juncture, occasionally they are invidiously saddled with the cruel label of "mid-list"—a term to be used with extreme caution around any working writer you may bump into at a social or any other sort of occasion. The irony consists of this: mid-career is often when some writers are just hitting their stride, taking chances as they've never done before, sometimes after composing books that never saw the light of publication, or whose first published works found a limited albeit admiring audience. This all takes place at the precise moment when publishers' gaze is drawn instead to the gleam of flashy, younger, emerging writers.

Again, at the risk of repetition: there's nothing wrong at all with embracing the *emerging*. Yet sign us up for the *emerged, still emerging*.

To be candid, though, literary prize–giving is not without its built-in complications and implicit pitfalls. The Simpson Project Committee is continually impressed by the finalists, including those not finally selected, and we look forward to the day when we will have additional prizes to bestow. In truth, passionate, full-throated advocates argued for every single extraordinary finalist on the shortlists of 2017 and 2018.

Literary notoriety sometimes, and not only in retrospect, baffles. The history of literary reception is full of examples of shooting stars who one day blink and disappear from sight, wunderkinder eventually forgotten, as well as so-called "writers' writers" who are unfairly neglected, or great authors who go unpublished or ignored, not to mention the late bloomers and the terminally overpraised. (And it's not exclusively the envious who keep a mental list of the overpraised.) For instance, if you find yourself in a slightly perverse mood, examine the list of Nobel Prize in Literature winners. You'll notice on the list no Mark Twain. No Henry James (who bored Clemens to tears of mockery). No Marcel Proust. No Virginia Woolf. No James Joyce. No Chekov, Lorca, Conrad, Nabokov, O'Connor, Borges, Roth, Oates, or Tolstoy. For the record, it was Tolstoy who asserted he was glad he didn't win because the money would only bring him "evil," thereby voicing a view never again to be uttered by a writer on planet Earth. And no thank you, I'm not going to touch the Bob Dylan subject. But I digress.

Everybody knows that a writer's life is not an easy one, across all levels. On perhaps the most mundane, the commercial, exist trials such as attracting an agent, coping with inevitable rejection, signing a book contract, getting reviewed, building an audience, negotiating entertainment rights (if one is lucky or unlucky enough, or possibly both)—each step potentially fraught. And yet writers write. Not that anybody asked them to, but that's beside the point, because maybe they should have been. Whatever the wellsprings of strength and intestinal fortitude, they are driven to create their stories, novels, poems, memoirs, essays, and their genre-crossed and genre-bending works. It's a choice, of course, and a vocation, and writers do what they do: they write. And if they are fortunate, they find an audience, sometimes small, sometimes impassioned. Not all writers are so fortunate, and many spend their entire lives toiling on the margins. The Project hopes to go some serious distance toward improving the lot of some of these eminently worthy emerged artists.

The Project intends to cultivate long-term, reciprocally beneficial relationships with Prize Recipients and Finalists, and to involve them in the University of California, Berkeley, and the Lafayette Library and Learning Center. All of them are warmly invited to read at featured Lafayette Library events, and former finalists are eligible to be considered for future prizes. Beyond that, broadly speaking, we hope the Simpson Literary Prize will give the recipients not only means to continue to grow, but the backing and confidence conveyed by our investment in them. Prize Recipients are publicly and privately celebrated at Berkeley and at the Lafayette Library. In addition, they are in brief but mutually enriching residence at the University of California, Berkeley, and the Lafayette Library and Learning Center. In this way we hope that they will have a dramatic, enlightening impact upon high school and university students, faculty, librarians, and readers and writers throughout the larger community, even while they themselves enjoy constructive engagement with new, appreciative audiences.

SIMPSON WRITING WORKSHOPS

We are all storytellers. From the first, we have been storytellers. Everyone knows this. We tell our tales and compose our poems all the time, however reflexively and casually. That is why the Project is grateful and pleased to be associated with high school-age writers. In our workshops, Simpson

Fellows (in concert with Simpson Prize Winners and the Simpson Project Writer-In-Residence whenever feasible) mentor young people, concentrating upon the art and the craft of writing across genres, including the short story and poetry, as well as autobiographical and nonfiction prose. Good and great things are conceivable when we instruct, encourage, and empower younger writers. We hope the accrued benefits of the Simpson Writing Workshops reverberate, and magnify, throughout their lives, whether or not they have the writer's calling or any literary ambition.

On this score, for instance, Noelle Burch, Contra Costa County librarian and coordinator of the Simpson Workshop at Juvenile Hall in Martinez, California, geared to young men who are incarcerated, shared her thoughts about the workshop:

The program gave the residents the opportunity to work one-on-one with Ismail [Ismail Muhammad, Simpson Fellow]*, where he led the residents through a series of activities and assignments which were designed to help them improve and develop their writing skills and foster creative thinking through writing prompts.*

Ismail was tremendously effective in assisting our kids in learning more about themselves through meaningful and therapeutic creative expression. Many participants used the opportunity to unpack complicated and sometimes sensitive personal topics that they may have never considered expressing through writing. As the workshops progressed, the kids began to feel more confident expressing themselves, and it showed through their work. Working with Ismail in this program has given these kids something that they might not have had before—an outlet to tell their stories, and a method to let them find their own voices.

It truly cannot be overstated how much an impact that the Simpson Family Literary Project has had with this program. It was an overwhelmingly positive experience, and has highlighted the importance of providing these kids an outlet that encouraged therapeutic expression through storytelling. As a librarian, I strive to provide opportunities that encourage these creative outlets, and aim to give my kids the resources that they need to better support their rehabilitation process. Both the teachers and probation counselors that I work with have noticed the profound impact that Ismail's programs have had on the kids, and have repeatedly told me how successful the workshops were in enabling the kids to speak freely and write from their heart.

Ms. Burch's take on the Project is essentially recapitulated by Girls Inc., located in downtown Oakland, California, and the comprehensive and diverse Northgate High School. As Lise Gaston, Simpson Fellow at Northgate, commented:

While I think they found the teaching of craft and genre helpful, the great benefit of the program was giving them readers, and a space to seriously discuss their writing. Though the skill of giving useful feedback was part of the learning process over the course of the semester, the act of sharing, of reading their work to each other in small groups, showed the writers' confidence and excitement at every stage. They also enjoyed "in class" writing exercises; they liked seeing their instructors participate alongside them, breaking down divisions between teacher and students: those moments where we could all simply be writers, working on our craft.

And here is Laura Ritland, Simpson Fellow at Girls Inc.:

Beginning with the descriptive language and poetry units first before moving onto fiction and memoir also seemed to be a great format for teaching these classes. The girls connected intimately with poetry as an expressive medium for their thoughts and feelings; it encouraged them to "open up," as one of the Girls Inc. instructors confirmed.

Julayne Virgil, CEO of Girls Inc., expanded on the point in *Oakland Magazine*: "Through the Simpson Family Literary Project the girls are exploring with a number of tools to express themselves and to understand others' experiences, building critical skill sets not only for their own personal and professional success, but also for their broader ability to connect with all of humanity."

What we see over and over again in our workshops is how creative writing connects students with each other and with their teachers, even as in a larger sense they bind extended families together over generations. Storytelling builds community, and awareness of shared experience, values, and aspirations makes for a vital, sustaining and sustainable culture. And when we attend to the emotional, intellectual, psychological, and artistic development of younger people, we can see firsthand how they begin to tap the power of the written word at their command. In the process, their personal growth fills us with hopefulness for them and their—and our—world.

The Simpson Family Literary Project, then, serves not only professional writers who have distinguished themselves in their art, but—just as central to our mission—the Project also serves educators who inspire and instruct new generations of readers and writers by creating conditions where creativity flourishes. Most importantly, The Simpson Project celebrates and supports new generations as they explore ways to express themselves creatively—to surprise and delight themselves and other writers and readers, exploiting their resourcefulness with language in stories and poems composed about their own lives and the lives of others.

THE PROJECT'S STORY

Indeed, the Simpson Family Literary Project has its own story to tell, and I'm positive it will turn out to be a pretty good one—except it isn't finished yet. As a work in continual progress, it's still coming together, and we're persistently reshaping and refining it—drafting and redrafting, cutting and revising, adding and subtracting as we go along. Honestly, part of me believes it may never be finished, which would be a most fitting result.

Some unfinished stories, of course, are never completed, and some are, for whatever reason, simply unfinishable. But that doesn't really describe ours. Our story starts and restarts, over and over, afresh with each workshop student, with each teaching Fellow, with each new work by a Simpson Prize Finalist and Recipient, with each talk and reading by the Writer-in-Residence, with each person attending our eagerly subscribed readings and events, with each reader of the authors we celebrate, with each high school and university student, with each librarian—with every person the Simpson Project strives to move, serve, educate, delight, and inspire.

Here's what I *can* say so far about our story. Ours is one story that takes on different shades of meaning with each telling, with the accents and emphases of each storyteller. Subtle complexities, nuances emerge for each creator and each listener. Upon reflection, this is understandable, and ultimately exhilarating. For the truth is, the Simpson Project is a story being told and retold by many in multiple circumstances.

Diverse narrators, characters, voices, styles, themes multiply, accumulate, meld, blend, converge. Scenes proliferate, settings flip, drama flourishes.

As we know, some stories are so appealing we never want them to end, we need to hear them again and again; just ask children at bedtime pleading again for a favorite tale, or readers who fall in love with a book and reread it repeatedly. That beloved book almost seems to metamorphose over the course of a reader's lifetime, or maybe it is that readers continually change and as a consequence they read it in a new way each time they longingly return.

"If a story begins with finding, it must end with searching." So says the philosopher and poet Novalis, in words the author Penelope Fitzgerald makes up in her novel *The Blue Flower*. Finding and then endlessly searching: that's what we do in The Simpson Family Literary Project. That is what storytellers do, too, and for a parallel reason. Restless and speculative, driven and probing, risk-taking and grounded: that describes our precepts as well as the participants who make the Project what it is today, and what it promises to be tomorrow.

One readily accessible place to read and hear *their* story, which is *our* story—in its continually starting over, continually finishing condition is right here where you are, in between and throughout the lines of the fictions, poems, conversations, and essays contained in the pages of this book.

◆◆◆

We love how some of our favorite stories begin: *Once upon a time.* That's one of the archetypal ways stories begin to take shape, whether it's implicit or explicit, and it's not exclusive to fairy tales' domain. There's something comforting, mysterious, and electrifying about that opening invitation into, and invocation of, the imagination, there's a promise implied and a covenant forged. It intimates for the listener, for the reader, I've got a tale to tell *you*, and when I'm finished you will be amazed, you will be stirred to insight, wonder, resolve, and action. If it happens to be a great story, afterward you may never be the same. You may not be able to adequately explain how you have changed, or why, but you will be changed nonetheless. This resembles a dream, only it's a *waking* dream. It's magic. It's a marvel. It's strange and familiar at the same time. It's a story. *And they lived happily ever after?* A drop-the-mic moment? I don't need to convince you that, for writers we cherish, it's usually somewhat more complicated and profound than that, with or without a mic to drop.

Our work is only possible thanks to the generous contributions of individuals, companies, and family foundations across the nation, all in support of the mission of the Project. Thank you for joining all of us—younger writers, professional authors, Simpson Fellows, professors and teachers and community leaders—as we tell our story. We invite you to add your ear, your eye, your voice, your heart, and your support to our tales from the Simpson Family Literary Project. We hope you yourself will become a *Simpsonista,* and make the Project's story your own.

To be continued.

Joseph Di Prisco
Editor
Chair, The Simpson Family Literary Project
August 2018

ACKNOWLEDGMENTS & NOTES

The Simpson Family Literary Project, simpsonliteraryproject.org

Grateful thanks extended to:

Authors and publishers for kind, generous permission to reprint.

The Lafayette Library and Learning Center Foundation. lllcf.org

The University of California, Berkeley, English Department, english.berkeley.edu

The University of California, Berkeley. berkeley.edu

The Contra Costa County Public Library. ccclib.org

2017 Simpson Prize Finalists—

T. Geronimo Johnson (Prize Recipient)

Valeria Luiselli

Lori Ostlund

Dana Spiotta

2018 Simpson Prize Finalists—

Ben Fountain

Samantha Hunt

Karan Mahajan

Anthony Marra (Prize Recipient)

Martin Pousson

Simpson Writing Workshops—

Contra Costa County Juvenile Detention, Martinez, California; Noelle Burch, Contra Costa County Public Library; Mt. McKinley High School, Contra Costa County Office of Education, Rebecca Vichiquis, principal; Ismail Muhammad, Simpson Fellow

Girls Inc., Oakland, Alameda County; Julayne Virgil, CEO; Laura Ritland, Simpson Fellow; girlsinc-alameda.org

Northgate High School, Mount Diablo Unified School District; David Wood, faculty; Lise Gaston, Simpson Fellow; northgatehighschool.org

PERMISSIONS

"Cityscapes in Mating Season" from Cityscapes in Mating Season by Lise Gaston, Signature Editions, 2017, reprinted with permission of the author.

"Clear as Cake," by Lori Ostlund, originally published in *ZYZZYVA*; reprinted with permission of the author.

"Cortés the Killer," by Samantha Hunt, originally published in *The New Yorker*, then included in *The Dark Dark*, reprinted with permission of Farrar, Straus and Giroux.

Hazards of Time Travel, by Joyce Carol Oates, excerpt from the novel, published by Ecco; reprinted with permission of the author.

How Stories Make the World: Bay Area Book Festival Panel Discussion—transcript printed with permission of the Bay Area Book Festival.

"Impasse Tempête," by Ben Fountain, originally published in *Ecotone*; reprinted with permission of the author.

"Last Words of Benito Picone," by Anthony Marra, originally published in *ZYZZYVA*; reprinted with permission of the author.

Poems by Geoffrey O'Brien: "Four Last Songs" (from *People on Sunday*); "D'Haussonville" (from *People on Sunday*), "Quick Trip" (from *Experience in Groups*), "Experience in Groups" (from *Experience in Groups*); reprinted with permission of the author.

Poems by Laura Ritland: "Garden Leave," "Interview with the Body," and "Marine Economy" from East and West by Laura Ritland are reprinted by permission of the author and Signal Editions/Véhicule Press.

"Revival Girl," by Martin Pousson, originally published in *Epoch*, then later in *Black Sheep Boy*, a novel-in-stories, reprinted with permission of Rare Bird Books.

UC Berkeley Commencement Address by T. Geronimo Johnson, printed with permission of the author.

"An Unbearable Tension: On James Baldwin and the Nation of Islam," by Ismail Muhammad, originally published in *Catapult*, and reprinted with permission of the publisher and the author.

Welcome to Braggsville, a novel by T. Geronimo Johnson; excerpted and reprinted with permission of HarperCollins.

"'A Wounded Deer—Leaps Highest': Motives for Metaphor," an essay by Joyce Carol Oates; reprinted with permission of the author.

Student Workshop Writings: printed with permission of the authors.

THE LAST WORDS OF BENITO PICONE

BY ANTHONY MARRA

2018 SIMPSON PRIZE RECIPIENT

It began in a hailstorm in 1975. Benito Picone trotted across Market Street, briefcase gripped overhead, shielding him from the falling sky and, inadvertently, the oncoming Buick. His legs buckled on the hood, his shoulder smashed spider webs into the windshield, and his arms pinwheeled as all 296 pounds of Benito Picone spun from the roof. He seized at the air. His briefcase burst in a cartoon flurry. Hailstones turned Market into a mile-long craps table. The fabric of his trench coat, suit coat, waistcoat, and trousers beat with the flapping of a hundred waiters laying tablecloths, and amid the fireworks flowering in the dark skies of his consciousness he did not once consider the heft of his body. Weightless for the first time in his life, he torqued in a horrible arc of beauty and landed in darkness.

When Benito woke, "My Favorite Things" from *The Sound of Music* was playing on the radio—*crisp apple strudel; doorbells; sleigh bells; schnitzel with noodles*—and he realized that the personal hell to which his immortal soul had been rendered sounded an awful lot like Austria. But he wasn't dead, not quite. A smock had replaced the herringbone three-piece he still wore weekdays, even though two months earlier he had lost his office lottery pool, his temper, and his job, in that order. The glossy bracelet on his wrist read St. Francis Memorial. Relief flooded the blue channels of his circulatory system. There was still time. He could still say his last words.

Over the years, Benito had paid much thought to his death. When he turned thirty, he began a nightly habit of recording his last words on a notepad in case he expired in his sleep: the end is a ballet without music or dancing; the end is relief. Benito had something, many things, in fact, to say about love and sorrow and pride and betrayal and forgiveness and beauty. The problem was that no one was the least bit interested in hearing them. Which made his last words a final chance to convert his failures into wisdom-building exercises, a last gasp to save himself from who he was. Who wouldn't want to listen to the final dispatch from a man walking over the edge? Whose ears wouldn't perk to hear one soul's answer to the question mark that punctuates every life? Those who had never paid him a moment's thought would lean in to hear what he had to say as he crossed over. Knowing this, knowing that a good ending can redeem a bad story, Benito had struggled to cram the sum self-knowledge of his thirty-nine years into a pithy single-sentence serving of wisdom that proved once and for all, to all the detractors, that Benito Picone did not live in vain.

"The end is a drizzly evening and I cannot take my umbrella with me," he said in Italian to the reticulated ceiling tiles. Not the most profound last words, but a good deal better than those of more celebrated lives (Conrad Hilton: "Leave the shower curtain inside the tub").

"That's no Spanish I've ever known." The sentence was pushed through the crooked maze of an East Coast accent. It came from the adjacent bed, where a woman propped on pillows observed him with her head at a skeptical tilt. She had the dazed pallor of a cave dweller dragged into daylight. Had Benito not just uttered his last words, he might have explained that Italian and Spanish weren't the same language, but you could spend a lifetime righting what Americans got wrong. He had only moments left.

Translucent tubes drew blood from one arm and streamed gray fluid into the other. A bleak epiphany: in the end, he was no more than a transit station for disturbingly opaque liquids. Beneath the gown, bruised continents had spread across his torso. His left leg lay in a splint and a fat foam noose halfheartedly strangled him. His abdominal organs felt composted. What had happened? He could only summon a dream of flying geese. Then a silver Buick, hailstones, his soul vacuumed into the sky.

A nurse entered. Benito turned as much as the beefy foam headlock would allow. "You're lucky to be alive," she said, ambivalently.

"But I'm dying," Benito clarified.

He hadn't set out to die that day, but now that it was happening, he received it as the arrival of a long-lost uncle he both loved and feared. He had no one on this side of the earth to say goodbye to, no one to write his obituary, no one to attend his funeral but a weak-chinned landlord who would probably reach into the casket to frisk his pockets for spare change. On the threshold now, he looked back and saw that the life he was leaving looked a lot like his apartment, a windowless cube of claustrophobia remarkable only for the reek of the litter box that doubled as an ashtray ever since his cat had left him. The oddly worded English emergency instructions alarmed through him: proceed to the exit as quickly as possible.

"Please, get a pen and paper," Benito entreated. "You must record my last words."

The nurse didn't move. She had a deadpan affectation, blunted over time by the nonsense of patients like Benito. The fatigue of a double shift was war-painted in purple beneath her eyes.

"My vitality is seeping from me!" he insisted. "I see a bright white light. I should move toward it, no?"

The nurse flicked the wall switch and the ceiling light went out. "That better?" she asked.

No, it wasn't.

"The light at the end of the tunnel may well be a sixty-watt incandescent," the nurse said, "but it's not the one over your head."

"But I'm dying," he said, more wish than lament.

"The worst you got is a broken leg, generally non-fatal among non-equines," she said.

"But I was hit by a car," he protested. "I was in a serious collision. I shouldn't be alive in this hospital room. I shouldn't be alive."

The nurse, in no need of further convincing, switched on the light as she left. The woman in the adjacent bed turned up the radio. It was Sonny Bono. Sweet mortality, come swiftly.

The next morning, Benito disappointingly awoke. The woman in the adjacent bed stared at him.

"Were you watching me sleep?" he asked.

"The TV's broken," she said.

She introduced herself as Marie. She had been orphaned at eleven and widowed at nineteen-year. She had no children and wanted none. After a childhood in Maryland and an adolescence in New Jersey, the palm trees lining the Embarcadero never failed to amaze her. She'd been brought in by a neighbor with alcohol poisoning. Her honesty unsettled Benito, who suspected that mental well-being depended upon a facility for selectively dismissing reality. At one point, she asked him what it had felt like, thrown from the launch pad of a windshield up into flight.

Benito tried to recall the pain, the shock, the pristine panic of the moment, but all he could remember was an eerie weightlessness. "Like swimming, maybe."

"Swimming?"

"What I imagine swimming feels like. I never learned to swim."

"Wait," she said. "You grew up on an island and you never learned to swim?"

Benito had already told her that as a boy he'd emigrated from Lipari, a barren volcanic island three hours by ferry north of Sicily.

"My mother was old world," he said. "To her mind, superstition was the only logic of an irrational world, and learning to swim would invite drowning as certainly as visiting the doctor invites disease. Her philosophy was that you had to surrender yourself to the Fates by not preparing for any disaster or misfortune, and that by offering your humility and powerlessness to them, they would keep you safe."

"And you still got hit by a car," Marie pointed out.

"In America, the Fates are more impressed with individual accountability."

"Is your mother in San Francisco?"

"She's dead," he said. He had been there when she went. Her last word had been his name. "Common cold became pneumonia. Never went to the doctor."

"Just because you're wearing a prophylactic doesn't mean your not getting fucked."

She had a point, but Benito wasn't sure exactly what it was. He readjusted his casted leg, but couldn't shake the memory of air, of weightlessness. He'd always wanted to learn to swim. A couple times, he'd signed up for lessons at the Presido Y, and had once even gotten as far as the locker room. But when he'd changed into his suit and taken an honest look at himself in the mirror, he'd immediately thrown his shirt back on.

"Do you swim?" he asked.

"In one liquid or another," she said.

By the third day, Benito conceded that his broken leg would only kill him if he were pursued by a large predator. The nurse informed the two patients that they would be discharged shortly. Neither had insurance and they were required to appear at the billing office before departing.

When the nurse left, Marie pulled the IV from her hand. She stripped her gown without turning away. She was androgynously streamlined, her whole body streaming from her clavicles like a coat from a hanger. Benito's shock (when had he last seen a woman naked?) rose to excitement (when had he last seen a woman naked!), which was immediately diluted by the realization that he was so insignificant a sexual being Marie hadn't even thought to close the curtain between them. She put on jeans and an oversized T-shirt that irresponsible wash cycles had thinned to a gauzy translucence.

"Let's boogie," she said.

Benito was unaccustomed to disobeying authority figures in uniform, even a nurse's uniform. He was even less accustomed to receiving invitations to boogie. He grooved on after her.

"Hurry up." She held open the emergency exit for him.

A broken leg seemed like a reasonable excuse for a limp, but a childhood of Catholic catechism and fascist schooling had conditioned him to submit to the imperative mood. The stairs stretched four floors. Benito gripped the handrail, gave his broken leg a tomcat lift, and pogoed down on his good foot. Two legs were barely enough to support all of Benito when he was at his best, and he hadn't been at his best since 1954. His one good leg was, as his father had once said of Benito himself, "nearly adequate." Marie wrapped his left arm over her shoulder. It seemed profane that she should place her lovely neck in the stockade of his unwashed armpit.

At the bottom of the stairwell, she snipped their hospital bracelets with scissors swiped from the nurse's station. Benito used Marie as a crutch as they crossed the lobby. The deeply engrossed security guard didn't peer up from his funny pages as they passed.

"Shall we?" Marie asked, opening the door to a parking lot blotched in gray puddles. They stopped under a tree. The leaves shivered with the breeze, spattering droplets on them. "Standing under a tree when it's raining keeps you dry. Standing under a tree when it's stopped raining keeps you wet," Benito said.

"That's some real deep shit." Marie rifled through her pockets, searching for bus fare. "You got any change?" she asked.

"Where are we going?" he asked. He had almost said you instead of we. They had shared a hospital room, but he wasn't sure they were ready to share the intimacy of a personal pronoun.

"You got any change?" she asked again, ignoring his question.

His pockets were empty, save for his apartment keys and a cemented wad of partially used tissues, but he patted them anyway. They had no money for a bus and took a taxi instead, hoping Marie's recluse neighbor would spot them the fare.

A quartet of sharp knocks startled Josef Lavrov from his nap. Marie, regrettably. She was his only visitor. He didn't like visitors. Whether the former had caused the latter was a matter great debate in 3C.

"I've brought company," Marie announced as he slid away the security chain. The poor man at her side was another flight of stairs away from cardiac arrest. His leg was casted in plaster and his voluminous thigh spilled over the top of the cast like a soufflé.

Marie made introductions before borrowing a few dollars to pay the taxi.

"My leg," Benito said. "I need to sit."

He locked eyes on Josef's most prized possession, a rococo Second Empire-style dining chair. Josef had found it in the window of a Haight Street consignment shop three months after his petition for political asylum had been cleared. Its dark hue bespoke Third World deforestation; its seat was goose down plumped in imperial purple velvet; its wooden back was calligraphically ornate. He had pressed his nose against the Haight Street shop window like a man checking his own vital signs, and found himself startling alive, incredulous that a chair built for royalty would be sold here, on the street, for anyone to buy. Nothing better embodied how far he'd come from the featureless furniture of his homeland. He had lived for that chair his first year in America, saving one of the four hourly dollars he earned folding fortunes into fortune cookies. Crest rail, ear, lancet arch, pierced slat, stile, quatrefoil, knee, cabriole leg, claw-and-ball foot: he learned the English words for every part of that chair before he acquired the vocabulary for half of what filled a grocery store vegetable aisle. On the first anniversary of his defection from the Soviet Union, Josef went to the consignment shop and bought the chair with ones and fives.

It was toward this treasured chair that Benito's wide posterior descended. Josef closed his eyes at the moment of impact. The chair hardly creaked, every bit the masterpiece the consignment store clerk had called it.

"Lovely old thing you have here," Benito said with a lilt to his accent that Josef couldn't identify.

"Benito. This is what? Spanish?"

"Why does everyone think I'm Spanish? Italian. As in from Italy."

"Ah yes," Josef said, snapping his fingers. "Of course, of course. With the pizza and the popes. Benito like Mussolini."

Benito looked like he'd been caught passing gas in a packed elevator. Josef was delighted. "I joke, I joke," Josef said. "But tell the truth, your father names you after the dictator, no? He wants for you to become strong leader, brave man, yaytsa big as oranges. Tell the truth, I am right, no?"

"I was born in 1935," Benito said softly. "Benito was a very popular name at the time."

Josef clasped his hands together, delighted by his discovery. "OK, OK. You are named after for Mussolini. In Italy, this is maybe very good. But not so much in America. Why don't you name yourself for Benjamin or Benny?"

"I considered it," Benito said. "But your name is your name. When Americans visited Italy in the 1930s, they had to change their names. Benny Goodman became Benito Bounuomo. Louis Armstrong became Luigi Braccioforte. It didn't seem any better doing the reverse."

"I am named Josef because my father had very much respect for Josef Stalin," Josef confessed. It wasn't the sort of thing he freely admitted, but he felt an affinity with this stranger who also bore weight of a tyrannical namesake.

Benito leaned forward, alert. "Well, you know, Stalin killed many more people than Mussolini ever did."

"Wrong side of history, right side of World War II," Josef countered. "Stalin was terrible, believe me, this I know. But Mussolini. He pals around with Hitler."

"Still, I think most people would agree that Mussolini was less evil than Stalin."

"Stalin destroyed fascism and saved civilization. Mussolini and Hitler played on the same Risk team. No comparison."

"Once I met an Adolf," Benito admitted, stretching his arms in a hoop above his head.

Josef whistled. "How about that. What was he like?"

"He had a complicated relationship with his parents."

Josef surreptitiously checked his watch. He suspected that Marie had taken whatever change was left over from the taxi fare, if she paid the fare at all, and had deposited it at the corner liquor store. But he wasn't willing to deprecate his neighbor in front of a man named after Mussolini.

Benito asked how he came to America.

"I am a defecator," Josef said. Benito frowned and studied the scuffed rim of his loafer. Perhaps he'd never met someone who had defected. Josef tried to put him at ease. "Don't be intimidated. It's not so glamorous or so dangerous."

"No," Benito said. "I wouldn't think so."

Josef went on. "Have you heard of Vyborg? No? Famous for its taproots and its proximity to the Finland border. So, in Vyborg I was a bus driver. Everyday I am driving the bus. I am a good bus driver, everyone knows this. So, one day the city transport director says, 'Josef, tomorrow are arriving some lackeys from the Ministry of Ferrous Metallurgy. You must drive them around.' I do not want to do this. I am very uncomfortable driving lackeys. But I say yes. That night, I am as flustered as a bird in a briefcase. What if the meetings go bad and they blame it on the bus driver? I do not sleep at all. In the morning, I take glass of brandy to sharpen my senses. No use. I doze off. Big crash. Blond people everywhere. Three broken road barricades. A mess."

"Wait. You drove into Finland?" Benito asked.

"First into Finland, then into the customs house. Embarrassing. So, I have two choices. Confess that I fell asleep while driving important lackeys. Lose my job. Maybe go to jail. International embarrassment.

Or, say I am defecting. Your Yogi Berra, he advises when you see the fork in the road, take it. So, I take it. Here I am."

Benito appeared genuinely impressed. "I just took a boat."

In truth, Josef had misjudged the military intelligence value of a municipal bus driver and the lifestyle he could expect in the West. He'd imagined America was filled with mansions and sports cars and fabulous wealth. It was, of course, they just didn't belong to him or anyone he knew. His only possession of true value was an old chair that a fat man was getting comfortable in.

A few minutes later, Marie returned with a brown paper bag in one hand. Josef's heart dropped a few centimeters. It was a lovely afternoon, the clouds were parting, this was no time to drink oneself to death. But all that emerged from the bag was a white bakery box looped in barber-pole twine.

"We're both named after dead dictators." Benito said, a trace of wonder to his voice.

"It's important to find your people," Marie said, and distributed napkins.

The three met again for pastries the following Wednesday. And then the Wednesday after, and the Wednesday after that. Over time, their Wednesday evenings became a small rise of elevation that their weeks ascended to and sloped from. In 1977, Josef bought two more Second Empire-style dining chairs from the Haight Street consignment shop. They sat in those chairs the week Benito announced he had found work and the week he announced he had been fired. They sat when Josef confessed he had skin cancer and they sat in the waiting room when the malignant tissue was removed. In autumn 1978, Marie believed she had bottomed out when she pawned her father's silver pocket watch, containing in its glass display the only image of her mother she'd ever seen. It took Marie all of 1979, 1980, and 1981 to string together a month of sobriety. One December she ornamented a plastic Christmas tree with all her twenty-four hour chips. On April 13, 1982, the anniversary of her first year sober, Benito and Josef gave her the pocket watch they'd bought back from the pawnshop. Marie opened it. The hazy photograph of her mother stared back but it was not her mother's love she felt in that room. She looked to the two men perched on chairs fit for beheaded French aristocrats. One smelled of mildew and still limped from the accident. The other treated the indefinite article as the great intellectual challenge of his life. If Marie had happier memories of family, she would have called them that. Together they went to movies, all-night diners, and once, in the balmy breeze of May 1988, to Reno, where they played penny slots and drank free fountain cola from plastic cups. In 1990, Marie taught Benito, at the age of fifty-five, to swim while Josef heckled from the bleachers. The cancer that had been removed from Josef's arms reappeared in 1999, and had already colonized bone, blood, and brain before it was discovered. He died in the St. Francis cancer ward two months later. Benito and Marie were just arriving as he left. His last word was hello. For an extra $800, the gravedigger buried him upright and uncasketed, enthroned in his favorite chair. Benito spent his mornings walking aimlessly through neighborhoods that seemed to get younger, richer, and whiter by the year. Youth, he'd heard, was a disorder generally cured by time; regarding the latter two, he was open to suggestions. The year, decade, century, and millennium turned over with the swipe of a second hand. He was sixty-five years old and had never used a computer. He was sixty-six, sixty-seven, sixty-eight, sixty-nine, seventy and he still had never used a computer. Wasn't life supposed to have a progression, a building toward something? Wasn't there a measurement beyond years to account for his time on earth? He didn't know, and that not knowing felt sunken in him like the footprints of something certain that had fled long ago.

On an April morning in 2015, Benito and Marie went to Pier 39 and watched sluggish sea lions spill into the water, their heads domed in sunlight. "What time is it?" Marie asked. Benito glanced to his watch, but couldn't speak. Invisible boulders pressed against his ribs. He raised a hand, the earth peeled away, blue sky everywhere. He was on his back now. Marie kneeled over him. She was pounding at his chest. He couldn't breathe. He must speak. He must say his final words. He'd been waiting his whole life for the opportunity. When he tried to speak, he found that her lips had sealed his. She was blowing air into his lungs. She was trying to breathe for him. It was so strange and unexpected a sensation—being breathed for—that he couldn't recall what he wanted to say. "Don't go, don't go, don't go," she pleaded. In all his years, he hadn't imagined that his last words would be spoken by someone else. He hadn't imagined he would die so loved. All around tourists flashed photos of the white-haired woman holding the dead man on that beautiful April morning.

WELCOME TO BRAGGSVILLE

A NOVEL

BY T. GERONIMO JOHNSON

2017 SIMPSON PRIZE RECIPIENT

Born and raised in the heart of old Dixie, D'aron Davenport finds himself in unfamiliar territory his freshman year at UC Berkeley. Two thousand miles and a world away from his childhood, he is a small-town fish floundering in the depths of a large hyperliberal pond.

(Excerpts)

D'aron the Daring, Derring, Derring-do, stealing base, christened D'Aron Little May Davenport, DD to Nana, initials smothered in Southern-fried kisses, dat Wigga D who like Jay Z aw-ite, who's down, Scots-Irish it is, D'aron because you're brave says Dad. No, D'aron because your daddy's daddy was David and then there was mines who was named Aaron, Doo-doo after cousin Quint blew thirty-six months in vo-tech on a straight-arm bid and they cruised out to Little Gorge glugging Green Grenades and read three years' worth of birthday cards, Little Mays when he hit those three homers in the Pee Wee playoff, Dookie according to his aunt Boo (spiteful she was, misery indeed loves company), Mr. Hanky when they discovered he TIVOEed Battlestar Gallactica, Faggot when he hugged John Meer in third grade, Faggot again when he drew hearts on everyone's Valentine's Day cards in fourth grade, Dim Ding-Dong when he undressed in the wrong dressing room because he daren't venture into the dark end of the gym, Philadelphia Freedom when he was caught clicking heels to that song (Tony thought he was clever with that one), Mr. Davenport when he won the school's debate contest in eighth grade, Faggot again when he won the school's debate contest in eighth grade, Faggot again more times than he cared to remember, especially the summer he returned from Chicago sporting a new Midwest accent, harder on the vowels and consonants alike, but sociable, played well with others that accent did, Faggot again when he cried at the end of *WALL-E*, Donut Hole when he started to swell in ninth grade, Donut Black Hole when he continued to put on weight in tenth grade (Tony thought he was really clever with at one), Buttercup when they caught him gardening, Hippie when he stopped hunting, Faggot again when he became a vegetarian and started wearing a MEAT IS MURDER pin (Oh yea, why you craving mine then?), Faggot again when he broke down in class over being called Faggot, Sissy after that, whispered, smothered in sniggers almost hidden, Ron-Ron by the high school debate coach because he danced like a cross between Morrissey and some fat old black guy (WTF?) in some old-ass show called What's Happening!!!, Brainiac when he aced the PSATs for his region, Turd Nerd when he aced the PSATs for his region, Turd Nerd when he hung with Jo-Jo and the Black Bruiser, D'ron Da'ron, D'aron, sweet simple Daron the first few minutes of the first class of the first day of college. Am I pronouncing that correctly? Yes, ma'am, Daron it is. What about this apostrophe, this light-headed comma? Feel free to correct me. Oh no, ma'am. Ignore that. It's all one word, ma'am. No need to call me ma'am. Yes, ma'am.

As was expected of Valedictorians, he had spoken of choices, though not his personal choices. His desk was stuffed tighter than a turducken with acceptance letters, but to list those would have been smug and boastful when most classmates were going to State or to stay. He instead pontificated on abstract opportunities to be grabbed, snatched out of the air like so many feathers, of the choices life extended to those who dared dream, of new worlds awaiting, of hopes to be fulfilled and expectations met, of how they would go forth and put B-ville, GA, squarely on the map. Never mind that it was ninety-two degrees, never mind that they could drink the air, never mind that, as Nana used to say, it was so greatly humid a cat wouldn't stretch its neck to lick its own juniors, he carried on about wishing over dandelions, and their delicate floating spores, and how they multiplied, superstitions taking seed even without belief—where he'd heard that he couldn't recall—and explained that our eyes move when we dream, and, lastly, with a smile advised the audience to, Always use sunscreen. His parting blow: an open invitation to visit him at *My future alma mater*, until then unknown to his father. Teachers applauded vigorously; peers clapped listlessly, more with relief than appreciation, but they didn't understand, and that was why he was glad to be leaving. He stepped from the podium a free man, at long last deaf to their tongues, and later thanked with aplomb the classmate who sidled up to the smoking steel drum and congratulated him on his engagement.

CHAPTER TWO

Of course there were the Bulldogs or the Yellow Jackets or the Panthers, or even the Tigers. And after a week as a Golden Bear, he wondered if one of those might have been a better choice. Long accustomed to the teachrt calling on him after his classmates proffered their feeble responses, D'aron sat in the front row but never raised his hand. He was not called on to moderate disputes, to weigh in on disagreements, to sagely settle debates. He was not called on at all, even when the subject in American History turned to the South, a topic on which he considered himself an expert, being the only Southerner in the class. (Not even when D'aron resorted to what the prof called a Horshack show.) The professor rationalized his reluctance to call on D'aron on such occasions as a resistance to essentializing. Said resistance D'aron found puzzling, and said affliction he apparently had developed no resistance to, constantly provoking the professor to ask, Am I the only Jew? Mika the only black? You the only Southerner? If the professor said he was Jewish, well, D'aron would take his word for it. Mika, though, was obviously the only black in class, and D'aron the only Southerner. Wasn't he essentially Southern? Wasn't that the core of his being, his essence, as it were? At least that was how he felt now that he was in California.

He held doors for the tender gender and all the elders. *Thank you* and *Please* and *May I* adorned every conversation. *Ma'am* was an escape artist extraordinaire, often slipping out midsentence. Professors wagged their fingers, but even the one who claimed it aged her, Only slightly less subtly but just as permanently as gravity, appeared at moments to relish this memento of a bygone era, this sole American who, like foreign students and athletes, recognized the instructors as ultimate authorities, approaching their bunkers as shrines bearing cookies and other gifts in outstretched hands, like a farmer leaving a peck of apples or a pair of just-plucked broilers at his lawyer's back door. Sir he could utter with censure.

Yet this inbred politeness was not what set him apart. Every student at Berkeley—all 36,142, he believed—played an instrument or a sport or volunteered for a social justice venture or possessed some obscure and rare talent. Or all four. Students raised in tents in Zimbabwe by field anthropologists and twin sisters who earned pilot's licenses at age fifteen and Olympians from as far afield as Norway. One student athlete, a track star, upon being asked, Are you considered fast in your country? smiled charitably, I am the fastest.

And the Asian students, he'd once confessed awe-stricken during a phone conversation with his mother, Some of the Asians, well, I shouldn't say some when they are a majority, but some of the Asian students speak multiple languages—more than a Holy Roller—languages I didn't even know existed. Kaya, in Cale Two, for example, is half-Korean but raised in Malaysia. She speaks Korean like her mom, Chinese like her dad, Malay like her cousins at home, and is already in French Two and Spanish Three. Does she even speak English? He sighed. Don't fret, honey. You earned the right to be there and you'll do fine DD baby. Don't fret. He murmured his thanks, reluctant to admit, let alone explain, that his distressed aspiration bespoke not lamentation but yearning. Kaya! Kaya mesmerized him, sitting in the basement commons study sessions twirling her hair around her pen as he wrote notes in Korean and IMed in English and tweeted in Malay, all while conjugating the subjonctif, her bare knees pressed together to balance a laptop surely hot to the touch.

Don't fret, his mom would repeat after his long silences. He didn't.

He didn't *fret*. Nor did he *reckon*. Or *figure*. Or *git*. Or study. Having followed his favorite cousin Quint's advice and picked a school more than a day's drive from home, he found the freedom intoxicating. If his parents could see him Monday mornings: tongue a rabbit's tail, stiff and bristly, D'aron not knowing whether to feel pride or shame. They guessed at it, though, after reading his midterm report. His mother, Are you sick, honey? His father, in the background, With alcohol poisoning maybe. (Following that call, D'aron changed his mailing address to the dorm.) But he didn't yet regret his decision to go westward-ho!

When he'd left home back in August to start school, Quint warned, Don't go ABBA or Tiny Dancer! Huh? Don't get gay. Don't get roofied and get made gay, either. Or, ho-mo-sex-u-al.

When he returned home for Thanksgiving, Quint squinted, You got AIDS? D'aron gave a lick and checked his reflection in his spoon, as if he hadn't only hours before, and every morning for that matter, paraded at length before the bathroom mirror in his skivvies. I can see your fucking ribs. You need a one-eight-hundred number. D'aron smiled. Without grits and waffles and hash browns and toast all at the same breakfast, and with walking everywhere, the famous freshman fifteen had gone the other way, but it looked and felt like fifty. Without the extra weight, he could finally confirm that his relatives weren't lying when they insisted he'd inherited his father's shoulders and forehead, and his mother's eyes and nose, and from them both a decent height.

And when he went home for Christmas, his aunt Boo teased, So you do have cheekbones. What are they feeding you, grass? You spent that money I sent you on crack?

Hey, hey, c'mon Auntie B.! Don't essentialize. All crackheads aren't skinny.

Is that a joke, Dookie? I got one for you. Hay is for horses!

He loved his family, but God he was glad they now lived so far away. Quint was at least right about that.

During those three years in special ed, I only missed the food. Quint paused. And tits. And of course my mom, she's mom, you know. And you, number one cuz. Exclamation point by way of a punch. But sure didn't miss all the yappity yip-yappity yap. And hunting. I missed hunting.

At least Jo-Jo, D'aron's best friend from high school, was happy for him. Jo-Jo patted his belly. I oughta go to college. That was a lot from him.

Chritsmas break didn't end soon enough. The morning the dorms opened, D'aron was on the ground in Cali three time zones away. It wasn't even the same country. By then he understood the geo-lingo. San Francisco was *The City*. Oakland was *O-town*, to be avoided at night—that was where the blacks lived—and the city of Berkeley was *Berzerkeley*, while Berkeley the school was *Cal*. The East Bay where Berzerkeley was located, supposedly suburban, felt plenty busy. Collectively, it was the Bay Area, a megalopolis—oh how that word polished his tongue—where the elsewhere unimaginable was mere mundanity.

Across the bay, The City convened in costume to race from bay to breakers. Happy meal toys and plastic bags were long outlawed and voters threatened circumcision and goldfish with the same fate. They'd once had a mayoral candidate named Jello. A roving band of Rollerbladers performed the "Thriller" zombie dance—that pop nativity—Friday nights in Union Square. And fuck, it was China in the airport. Yet The City thought Berzerkeley was weird. D'aron thought it was beautiful, never mind the nag champa, never mind the crusty hippies and gutter punks in greasy jackets stiff as shells lined up on Telegraph Ave hawking tie-dye and patchouli and palming for change. On clear days, a pageantry of wind and water under sun, the bay a sea of gently wriggling silver ribbons, and the Golden Gate hovering in the distance like a mystical portal. East of campus lazed tawny hills. On foggy days blinding bales of cotton candy strolled the avenues dandy while in the distance the tips of the bridge towers peeked through the mist like shy, gossamered nipples. The Bay Area was a beautiful woman who looked good in everything she wore.

What has intimidated him those early weeks of his freshman fall semester felt like home during his second semester—freshman spring. The clock tower known as the Campanile rose from the center of the campus with the confidence of the Washington Monument, marking time in style, and on the hour, music students sounded melodies on the carillon. He often lunched alone at the base of that monolith, on the cool stone steps, facing the water due west, attention drifting with the lazing waves and the steady stream of Asian students moving—no, migrating—between the library and the engineering buildings. As he worked up the courage to wander farther from Sather Gate, the symbolic campus border, he discovered Indian, Vietnamese, Mexican, Thai: tastes luring him deeper and deeper into a town of Priuses and pedalers, both of which yielded patiently to pedestrians. Laid back, liberal, loose. The locals' mantra, No worries; the transplants' motto, It looks like a peninsula but feels like an island.

UC BERKELEY ENGLISH DEPARTMENT COMMENCEMENT ADDRESS

MAY 20, 2017

BY T. GERONIMO JOHNSON

2017 SIMPSON PRIZE RECIPIENT

Does it feel real yet?

Greetings, faculty, administration, guests, graduates. It's a pleasure to be here.

It's a joy to stand before my fellow readers, writers, lovers of literature, word nerds, Golden Bears, travelers on the journey toward justice. (Hold on, I got you.) I am so happy for you. I am happy for the world that is receiving you.

Commencement calls for advice, so let's get that out of the way. Friends, I stand before you as a novelist, but I served time in finance. Be prudent in your use of credit, every loan is a mortgage on your future. Think of credit as a simple machine: it can be a lever or a screw. I'm sure you know which machine you want. That's the only piece of advice I'll offer today.

I propose that the topic of the day is simple: How will we obtain the transcendent unity necessary to ensure the survival of the species? Before we answer that, though, I want to be your hype man.

These graduating scholars have proven their mettle in the number one English department in the country, in the top-ranked public school in the world. It's not easy. (Am I right?) And in doing so these graduates, each and every one, have demonstrated astounding moral and intellectual courage.

On my cue, I ask you to give them a deafening round of applause, a ridiculously loud round of applause. They have earned that, and more.

I would like everyone to cheer for these graduates as if our lives depended on them, *because they do*. I am not saying this only to assure you of money well spent. Thank you.

Now I want to address not the graduates but their guests.

Friends, these graduates hail from all around of the earth, and have assembled here on this campus to study *English*. What does that mean? There is no shortage of jokes that run something like this: Soooo, you're earning a degree in the language you were born speaking.

But what does it mean to study literature, to take a degree in English. It means they embody this university's very motto and reason for being. Berkeley's motto is "Fiat Lux." Let there be light. That light may be born of a fire, a distant star, a valiant spark, a neural connection. I assert that these graduates are humanity's light bearers—one and all.

What exactly do they do: the surfeit of neologisms, critical theory, all those confounding French thinkers—it may seem very arcane and esoteric, but I assure you it is not. To illuminate their generous contributions—past present and future—I want to talk a little bit about story, a particular story.

I want to talk about *The King in Yellow*, the short story collection by Robert Chambers. In the second story, the narrator visits his friend Boris, a sculptor and self-taught artist. Boris and the narrator are two points of a love triangle, and the third point, Genevieve, is deeply depressed. Boris, perhaps in an effort to impress Genevieve, has developed a solution that instantly fossilizes organic material. When the narrator arrives on the scene, Boris places a fresh lily into a solution, and from the basin withdraws a statue in the shape of that same lily. The author writes: "The marble was white as snow, but in its depths the veins of the lily were tinged with palest azure, and a faint flush lingered deep in its heart." And later on that page, Chambers writes: "from somewhere within came a rosy light like the tint which slumbers in an opal."

The alchemical transformation leaves the living thing dead, at first glance. The essence of the lily's form is frozen in stone, except for this heat that remains at the center of the petrified object. That is precisely what literature is—an amplification of inner light, of the rosy glow, the spark we all carry within. Behind the theory, behind the writing, behind the alphabet itself, behind the 0s and 1s—if you read e-books—is simply this incessant insistent glow—story. We do not DO films, blogs, westerns, romances, Amazon miniseries. We DO story. Humans cannot survive without story anymore than they can survive without sunlight.

Story is so powerful that in this age of scientism, when statistics have taken on an aura of mysticism, people are still constructing story. And even though many tech fans cheered after Google's Artificial Intelligence defeated the human Go champion, even more tech fans cheered when an AI who later named itself Benjamin wrote a screenplay. And when you hear grumbling and glee about big data, you hear analysts reading and writing new stories for us. And political discourse has been reduced to a Battle Royale of adrenalized narratives. And any time you are exposed to publicity, you are exposed to a story.

So those bedtime stories we tell children, and the stories of mourning and celebration we share with friends and loved ones, and all those advertisements, and all these tweets—THE TWEETS—are all thrown into the same soup. Which ones should we listen to? Which ones do we listen to? Unfortunately, all, because story grafts itself onto our very being. There is no inoculation against it, hence the weaponizing of narrative in the political arena.

Milan Kundera believes that every great philosophical idea appears first in a novel. I almost agree. I take that to mean that every great philosophical idea was first transmitted between humans in the form of a story. For example, in *The Odyssey*, after blinding the Cyclops Polyphemus and smuggling his crew out of that cave, Ulysses tells Polyphemus:

Cyclop! if any, pitying thy disgrace. Ask, who disfigured thus that eyeless face? Say 'twas Ulysses: 'twas his deed declare, Laertes' son, of Ithaca the fair.

At that moment, Ulysses, the son of a man, tells Polyphemus, son of Neptune, that a child of a god has been bested by a child of a man. This assertion of the role of humanity—and our agency on earth, and our relative link on the great chain of being—is central to our modern world, whether written or shared beside a fire.

And in *The Outline of History*, H. G. Wells writes: "Human history becomes more and more a race between education and catastrophe." I ask you today, friends, what converts catastrophe into education? What converts the execution of a man into a religion, what converts a troubled history of genocide and colonialism into a legend of discovery and triumph, what converts the innocent into the guilty and vice versa. It is story.

But what exactly is story? The word derives from the Latin verb *narrare*, "to tell", which is derived from the adjective *gnarus*, "knowing" or "skilled." We know our world and ourselves though our stories. But more importantly, story is our defense against the chaos of unknowing. The word "religion" stems from the Latin *religare*, to bind. This has traditionally been taken to mean that our shared religious values bind us into communities of practice. I, though, take this to mean that our religious narratives bind an otherwise chaotic world into an apprehend-able experience. It is this story-telling custom which keeps us whole, keeps us human.

Imagine our early ancestors, battling the elements, engaged in a struggle to carve life out of a world where death offers not even a trigger warning. At the rugged shores charged by the bitter sea's relentless surge, on the arid sands combed by mad, blind winds, and on towering, craggy peaks sculpted by dark heaven's fusillades, who did humans first encounter and find unyielding? Facing a volcano, a razor clawed feline, an earthquake. How did we make sense of this? Through stories that became the myths and legends that continue to influence us today.

And before my nephew goes to sleep, like many children, he demands a story. My newborn daughter demands only to be fed, and I can't help much there. My nephew needs this story, even if he has heard it before. And while there are reams of research to explain why children enjoy repeatedly reviewing the same stories, when I watch him resist sleep's sly machinations, wrestle those heavy paws, dodge slumber's embrace, I am reminded of, and sense in him, the improbable weight of nothingness, the void beyond us, what we cannot see and cannot know, the absolute terror and mystery and joy of human existence, a fundamental anxiety we abate with drugs, sex, ritual, television, shopping; technology; an anxiety we have for millennia combatted and commanded and restrained through story.

We tell stories around the fire, but what I am telling you is that story is that fire. Story made that fire possible. Story as fire brings to mind Prometheus, and Prometheus may be our rightful muse because to bring fire to earth is to illuminate life. And when I come to illuminated life, it is time to talk about not only story, but also literature. Literature, like photography, slows life down long enough for us to grasp and examine thoughts, feelings, and impressions that might otherwise remain gauzy intuitions. This slowing down, this fixing in amber, this preserving is crucial. For how else would we know others—others are too mercurial for us to fully grasp them, even if only because our own personalities and perspectives are mercurial as well. And how else would we know experiences that we have not had firsthand? Simply put, life's architecture is articulated, too fluid and dynamic to be fully grasped by the sense organs. So we need story—as literature.

And as we age and mature, and ossify, how else do we preserve "the faint flush lingering deep within our own hearts," which takes us back to *The King in Yellow*. The character Boris, whose solution instantly fossilizes organic material, is described in the book as a chemist. Nowhere is alchemy mentioned, and yet when describing the scene, I referred to the "alchemical transformation." I did so because alchemy is a metaphor for the transformation of the soul, and of all the arts, because literature is the most intimate, it is literature and the process of engaging and being engaged by it that comes closest to alchemy. There is in alchemy a process known as palingenesis or the creation and recreation of life from matter previously rendered inert. This is literature: the universal and the particular of the human experience, are reduced to language and that language resurrected in the reader's mind as an experience that enthralls and transforms. Through words.

The world is built of words and not things.

At the end of *The King in Yellow*, we learn that the fossilizing effect is not permanent, though it lasts enough to suggest otherwise. Eventually, the housekeeper finds goldfish floundering on the floor beneath a mantle where two statues of goldfish once stood; and a room that held a statue of a rabbit is now home to warm, happy bunny, and, what I did not tell you was that Genevieve, in a fit of despair, had thrown herself into a pool of the solution, but now awakes in the cemetery under the watchful eye of the Madonna. How they are different—the goldfish, the rabbit, Genevieve—we are not told, but we imagine that they are, that they are changed—through their time as, with, and in, story. Transformed by the faint flush.

Literature is that light. In an era, and area, where immense resources are being invested in dangerous simulacra, these graduates are the guardians of that tradition. They are the stewards of our humanity.

When I originally conceived of this speech, I intended to sidestep politics. I saw no point in telling you what already know. I saw no need to repeat and regurgitate the wholly unoriginal predigested disingenuous political "analysis" with which we are daily assaulted via screens large and small. But I was made to believe that you are more than amenable to such engagement. In other words, I was told that this was not the perfect Arts and Science's commencement speech because it didn't say anything about Putin or Conway, or Bannon, or Sessions, or prison, or getting drunk.

First, you can sleep well tonight knowing that Dwayne Johnson, aka The Rock, is leading in the 2020 presidential polls. So ends the good news. No, you graduates, are the good news.

The night of the election I was at a residency in Oregon. After votes were tallied, I witnessed vomiting, soul-wrenching sobs, and the beginnings of a miscarriage. A life at risk. The ship of democracy had run aground upon a shoal of doom, and an apocalyptic anxiety took hold as fires long raging in the boiler room ate their way to the observation deck.

Yet fire cleanses. Mt. Fuji, the tallest mountain in Japan and a sacred pilgrimage destination, believed to be named after a Buddhist Fire god, Fuchi, was formed by series of violent volcanic eruptions that occurred over a 100,000–year period. The venerated summit, fortified by each inferno, was immortalized in a series entitled *36 Views on Mt. Fuji.*

I've written thirty-six views on the new administration, and our explosive political atmosphere, and I'll share most of them.

1. Much of your success will be the result of sheer will. If you lacked that, you wouldn't be sitting here.
2. In "Pride," Kendrick Lamar writes: "I'll make schools out of prison."
3. In Song IV of *The Consolation of Philosophy* Boethius writes: "Nothing can subdue Virtue."
4. Defeat begins in the mind. To submit to despair is to tender your own ruination.
5. We, as a species, have missed several dinner dates with doomsday. Consider the Jewish revolt against the Romans in 66–70 AD, Y2K,

the Mayan prophecy. The list goes on. Yet here we remain, with our student loans, melting ice caps, and Steven Seagal—because the Ukraine doesn't want him (at least not for five years).

6. With the exception of Fox news reports, nothing could be farther from the truth than to fear that the current administration heralds an apocalypse of any kind.

7. Our reigning apocalyptic anxiety is a metaphorical affliction born of a binary morality, informed by Christian eschatology, aggravated by the Western notion of linear time, and, most importantly, inculcated through fear—a calculated inculcation of fear. I suggest we radically revise our worldview, our sense of personal power, and our relationship to language, and by language I mean the entire supra-semiotic domain: word, image, gesture.

8. We must reconsider—to paraphrase our own George Lakoff—the metaphors we live by. Are we establishing our own, or are other folks foisting their metaphors upon us. If so, are us accepting them?

9. Sometimes we forget that this country has been struggling toward perfection since its inception. As Tocqueville says, "When the past no longer illuminates the future, the spirit walks in darkness." Let's travel back in time to world before November 8, 2016 to keep this in perspective.

10. In 2015, the National Center for Trans Equality conducted a nationwide survey. They learned that trans folks were more than twice as likely as the US population to be living in poverty, and trans folks of color, were up to three times as likely as the US population to be living in poverty. The unemployment rate among transgender people of color (20 percent) was four times higher than the US unemployment rate, 5 percent. And I'm not even going to talk about the frequency of violent assaults, including murder.

    a. What I am telling you is that we are always fighting.

11. Our prison population swelled under a tremendously popular democratic president.

    a. What I am telling you is that we are always fighting.

12. In 2015, 89 percent of colleges reported zero rapes. Key word: *Reported*.

    a. What I am telling you is that we are always fighting.

13. In 1993, the man who founded the Federation for Immigration Reform as well as the Petoskey chapter of the Sierra Club, wrote in a letter to a colleague, "I've come to the point of view that for European-American society and culture to persist requires a European-American majority, and a clear one at that."

    a.   What I am telling you is that we are always fighting.

14. Promise Keepers, whose ensign is spookily similar to an Army Ranger patch, and the rest of the constitutional refuseniks are nothing new either.

    a.   In 1868 a benevolent organization was chartered:

    b.   To protect the weak, the innocent, and the defenseless from the outrages of the lawless;

    c.   To protect and defend the Constitution of the United States;

    d.   To aid and assist in the execution of all constitutional laws.

15. That benevolent institution formed to protect the weak and safeguard the constitution is known today, as it was then, as the Ku Klux Klan.

    a.   We cannot attribute that to this administration.

    b.   This administration owns the patent on none of their ideas.

    c.   What I am telling you is that we are always fighting.

16. In other words, if tomorrow we awoke with a Westminster parliamentary system and our legislators passed a resolution of No Confidence, we would immediately be cured…of nothing…of absolutely nothing. But if we could be "cured," how would we react to the news that approximately every twenty-eight hours a trans person is killed somewhere on this earth, often in some public location. Would we glue haunch to couch, Netflix and chill, or would we be outraged enough to do something about that as well?

17. American history is a cruise ship docked in the port of today. Some passengers disembark having spent luxurious hours on the sun deck and at the seafood buffet while others have been so far below decks for so long that they have no idea we are even at port.

18. If we say that this is the worst it's ever been, we discount the experiences of many Americans who will tell you that life here has always been a struggle.
19. I say this not to discourage you but to encourage you, to remind you that, as Reverend King said, "The arc of history is long."
20. This country holds today every promise it ever held, and, as has always been the case, those promises are seeded in our hearts and will be brought to flesh only if we are committed to engaging fully in our lives.
21. We must keep in mind an adage I paraphrase here: To win a battle in the north, start a fire in the south.
22. The endless pathologizing of the administration is a game, their game, and it is a lethal distraction. A diagnosis is not a cure. We can react to alarming tweets, or we get ahead of them.
23. Our greatest risk is the adoption of practices and behaviors that betray our values.
    a. You must be an evangelist for hope.
    b. Proselytize for empathy and charity.
    c. This may not be wanted you wanted to hear, but it's incumbent upon the offended to educate the offender. You know this.
24. Outrage or fear or distress IS the call to action. Wonder not what to do. The starting point is simple: Make no distinction between your personal and political selves because they are the same. We have been told all our lives to avoid discussing in mixed company politics, money, or religion—but those are the three arms that crank the wretched machinery in which we presently labor.
25. We are looking up expectantly when we should be thinking laterally. It is always in our power to help another human being and change the world. In fact, it is only in our hands. We are coauthoring this world. Remember the Birmingham Children's Crusade. Those were high school kids, some even younger.
26. We must not give up. We must not become language apostates. We are suffering an epidemic of miscommunication within families.

27. Since the election, many white people have told me that they are no longer talking to their families. That's not helping.

   a. It's also one reason, when Obama was elected, there were approximately 191 patriot groups and militias were operating domestically, but by 2011 there were 1608.

   b. The only weapon they cannot confiscate is your heart.

   c. If white people will not talk to white people about racism, and men to men about sexism, and heterosexuals to heterosexuals about homophobia, we surrender the power to leverage homogeneity in the service of heterogeneity.

   d. It is incredibly hard to talk peaceably to those with whom you violently disagree, but community and communication and connection is the only cure.

28. In a pan-African occult text it is written: There are no concrete realities called "medicines" and "poisons." There exist medicinal relations and toxic relations.

   a. Martin Buber wrote: "A soul is never sick alone, but there is always a betweenness also, a situation between it and another existing human being." If, as Buber suggests, maladies of the soul are not borne in solitude, neither are its ecstasies and educations.

29. And one of these ecstasies, educations, and avenues of betweenness is *art*, especially literature. You are schooled in this. You are equipped to change minds and hearts. Your degree confers upon you all the "rights and privileges pertaining thereto." Mentally pencil in this edit: *rights privileges and responsibilities*.

30. Remember that imperialism has always been buttressed by false empiricism. The history of European colonial expansion is inextricably tied to an interlocking system whose components we have only recently begun to define as white supremacy, patriarchy, and pseudoscience.

31. So we face the truth and work harder because this is not the end, but a new beginning.

32. We have the chance to make the country great for the first time. Not great again but *great for the first time.* Because for many it never was.

33. Embrace this occasion with all your might. This is what we do. We struggle, always, and forever until all people everywhere are free.

34. Ask yourself this: *What converts catastrophe into education?* The answer is inside of you.

35. Darkness is not intractable. It quails at light.

36. Fiat Lux. *Fiat Lux!*

CLEAR AS CAKE

BY LORI OSTLUND

2017 SIMPSON PRIZE FINALIST

Marvin Helgarson smoked a pipe. When he listened to us, he nipped at the pipe—*pah, pah, pah*—the way that people who smoke pipes do, and when he told us things about our writing, he jabbed the pipe in the air for emphasis. I liked Marvin Helgarson. He was tall, not just everyday tall but tall even by Minnesota standards, though that's not why I liked him. I'm just trying to give details, what Marvin Helgarson called "salient features."

The class met Tuesday evenings in the Humanities Building library, sixteen of us wedged in around two long wooden tables that came together in a T with Marvin Helgarson at the head. It felt like Thanksgiving the first night, all of us too close together and filled with dread, though later, after Marvin Helgarson explained about perspective, I could see that maybe that was just my perspective.

"Liars and thieves," said Marvin Helgarson to get things going. "That's what you get with a room full of writers." He rose and swept out his arms like Jesus to include us all.

He meant it as an icebreaker, and most of us chuckled, but the woman across from me said, "Oh dear. I didn't know anything about that"—meaning, I guess, that she had a different idea about writers and writing, a different idea about what she had signed up for. Her name was Wanda, and she had large warts on her chin and cheeks, and later these warts would appear on the characters in her stories. We were always nervous about discussing them, worrying, I suppose, that we might read something into the warts that Wanda had not intended and that she would know then what it was that people saw when they looked at her.

"Wanda," said Marvin Helgarson, "I don't mean writers are really thieves." He paused, picked up his pipe, and sucked on it. "It's more like when someone lends you a pen to use, and then you just don't give it back." About lying, he said nothing.

"You're going to be working together intimately," Marvin Helgarson said, "so you need to know who you're dealing with." He asked for a volunteer to begin the introductions, and Fred Erickson, who was wearing a tie with a treble clef on it, jumped right in, describing his family and hobbies and years as the director of a choir in Idaho, from which he was now retired. Idaho seemed far away to me, and I wondered how he had ended up in Moorhead, Minnesota, but I didn't ask because I was intimidated by my classmates, most of whom came to campus once a week for this class but were adults with jobs and families the rest of the time.

I took a lot of notes that semester, tips that Marvin Helgarson shared to help us with our writing, like when he told us that sometimes the things that seemed most compelling to write about should not really be written about at all. They were just anecdotes, he said, odd things that had happened to us that were interesting to discuss in a bar but were not literary, by which he meant that they could not *transcend the page*. He explained this the first night of class, jabbing the air with his pipe so that we understood it was important, and then he said it again several months later when we discussed the nutty lady's story about a woman who cleaned rest stops along I-94. In the story, the woman and her cleaning partner were finishing the rest area near Fergus Falls when they discovered a body inside one of the trashcans. The story, which was just two pages long, mainly a lot of boring details about cleaning that lent veracity, ended like this: "The woman was dead and she was also naked. We were shocked and scared, and after the police came, we finished the bathrooms and went home."

When Marvin explained to the nutty lady that it wasn't really a short story, that it was more of an anecdote, she stood up. "Anecdote?" she said. "This really happened, you know. It happened to *me*, right after my ass-wipe husband left, and I had to be at that job every morning at six." She snorted. "Anecdote." Then, she walked out. It was late, nearly nine o'clock, and we could hear her footsteps echoing, not only because the building was empty but because she was wearing ski boots.

We didn't see the crazy lady again, but at the beginning of the next class Marvin showed us what she had left in his mailbox: a manila envelope with our stories for the week, chopped into strips with a paper cutter. You see, she really was crazy. But also, she'd had enough of us I think, enough of us telling her stuff about her writing. Three weeks earlier, she'd submitted a story about a woman whose vagina hurt all the time, except when she was having sex. As a result, her husband, who was a farmer, got very tired of having sex all the time and told her that she needed to go to the doctor to have her vagina checked. "I'm putting my foot down" is what he said, which made me laugh, though I didn't say so because I didn't think the story was supposed to be funny.

The woman and her husband spoke with what seemed like Irish accents, but when they drove into town to see the doctor, they drove to Bemidji, which is in Minnesota. I raised my hand and said they sounded Irish, pointing to things like "lassie" and "thar" because Marvin had told us to back up our comments with examples from the text, but the crazy lady looked pleased when I said they sounded Irish. "Yes," she said. "They're from Ireland. They moved to Minnesota when they were young in order to have an adventure and be farmers and also because something tragic happened to them in Ireland and they needed a fresh start."

"I guess I missed that," I said and began shuffling back through the story.

"No," she said. "It doesn't say it. It's just something I know. I was creating a life for my characters off the page, the way that Marvin said we should."

"That's a lot to have off the page," pointed out Thomas in what I thought was a very nice voice. Thomas was also one of the older students in the class. The first salient feature about Thomas was that his parents met at a nudist colony, where they were not nudists because they worked in the kitchen, chopping vegetables and frying meat. The other salient feature about Thomas was that he was a minister. I knew these things because he sometimes wrote his sermons at Jack's, the bar that I hung out at and one night we drank a pitcher of beer together and talked, but when we saw each other in class the next week, we both felt awkward.

"But the story isn't about them leaving Ireland," said the crazy lady triumphantly. "It's about"—she paused because I guess even a crazy lady feels strange saying "vagina" to a minister—"the pain in her female parts."

None of us knew what to say, so we looked down at the story, at the scene in which the woman and her husband, who was tired from having sex all the time, visited the doctor. When she was in the doctor's office, lying on the table with her feet in the stirrups, the doctor, who was an elderly man, positioned himself between her legs and called out, "Three fingers going."

This was supposed to be a minor detail I think, but Tabatha, who was a feminist, got mad. "That's ridiculous," she yelled at the crazy lady. "What kind of a doctor would say, 'Three fingers going'?"

"Doctors are just regular people," the crazy lady yelled back. "They get tired of saying the same things over and over, day after day. This doctor is like that. He's old, and he's tired. I am showing that he's a regular person who is exhausted and wants to retire. I am developing his character."

"That's not development," Tabatha said. "Then the story becomes about him, about how he's a misogynist and is going to get sued one of these days for saying things like 'three fingers going' to women when they're in a vulnerable position."

Tabatha was not someone that I wanted to be friends with, but I liked having her in class because she never disappointed me. Her first story, called "Cardboard Jesus," was about this guy Bart who spends all day watching television, and then one day a cardboard man jumps out of the TV and starts going on and on about how Bart needs to change his life, so Bart names the little man Cardboard Jesus. Finally, Bart gets tired of Cardboard Jesus making him feel bad about his life, so he puts Cardboard Jesus in the garbage disposal. The story ends with Cardboard Jesus getting chewed up, and the last line is him calling out from inside the disposal, "Why hast thou forsaken me?"

Most of us did not really care for "Cardboard Jesus." I said that it seemed unlikely, and Marvin said, "Are we talking character believability?" and I said that I couldn't really put my finger on it but that there wasn't a character worth *rooting for* in the whole piece. Tabatha snorted and said, "It's not a football game," even though we weren't supposed to talk when our story was being discussed.

"Maybe it's the dialogue," I said finally.

Just the week before, Marvin had explained about dialogue, how it's supposed to sound like a normal conversation except less boring. Our dialogues, it turned out, had too much verisimilitude. "Look," Marvin had said. "Imagine a guy goes into McDonald's and says, 'I'd like a Big Mac and fries,' and then the cashier says, 'Okay, that'll be $4.05,' and the guy pays and walks out with his burger and fries." He paused. "Typical conversation, right?" and we nodded. "So what's wrong with putting that conversation in a story?" he asked.

Tabatha's hand went up. "Why is everything always about McDonald's?" she said. "I would never have that conversation because I would never go to McDonald's." She looked around the table. "Or Burger King," she added, preempting the possibility of a setting change.

Marvin Helgarson sighed. "Fine," he said. "But my point is that this conversation is only interesting if one of them says something we don't expect, if the cashier says, 'No, sir, you may *not* have a Big Mac and fries.' Then you have a story." Tabatha started to speak, probably planning to point out that the cashier was doing the man a favor, but Marvin held up his hand at her. "Dialogue," he explained, "is all about power shifting back and forth." His pipe volleyed illustratively through the air.

"What's wrong with my dialogue?" Tabatha asked, looking at me and making her eyes small.

"I don't know," I said. Her dialogue was the opposite of what Marvin had cautioned us about. It didn't have any verisimilitude. "I guess it just feels sort of biblical."

The crazy lady raised her hand and said that there was nothing biblical about the story. She said the story was libelous, and Marvin said, "I think you mean blasphemous," and she said that she knew what she meant and so did God. Thomas said nothing, even though he was a minister, and then Tabatha announced that everyone had missed the point, which was that "Cardboard Jesus" was a "modern-day crucifixion story."

Each Sunday after church, my parents called my dorm room, my mother dialing because the telephone made my father nervous. Though only a week had passed since the last conversation, my mother always had plenty to say because my mother was the sort of person who conversed in details. She began with who had been in church that morning, and who had not, and why, and moved on to what types of bars and cookies were served during the coffee hour afterward, and from there, to what she planned to serve with the ham that was baking in the oven at that very minute. Then, she broadened out to cover the specifics of the preceding week: what they had eaten for supper each night and what illnesses had beset the town. During these conversations, I often became abrupt with my mother, though she seemed not to notice, for I do think that it occurred to her, ever, that I was not interested in these details, all of them adding up to a life that I did not want.

Of course, there was more to it than that. I had stopped believing in God. I didn't even know when it had happened, just that one day I understood that I did not, almost the way that you look out the window and realize the leaves are gone yet you can't remember seeing a single one fall. I had told no one, certainly not my parents, who would have said, "Well, what do you expect?" and then prayed for me, which I did not want.

"There are no saints or sinners," Marvin Helgarson had taken to saying when he criticized a character for being what he had, at the start of the semester, called "cardboard" but switched to calling "two-dimensional" after Cardboard Jesus. "None of us is all bad—or all good." Unlike Marvin Helgarson, my parents did believe that people could be all good; in fact, they believed not only that people could be all good but that they should be. My parents did not think that people's weaknesses were interesting or literary. They just thought that weakness led to sin.

Eventually, my father would demand the receiver. "Not much to report," he would say, and I would reply, "Me neither," and then he would ask something general about my classes and something specific about my bank balance, and as he prepared to hand the phone back to my mother, he would add, "Remember, Renee, communism is Satan at work," the way that other parents, I imagined, might admonish their children to study hard.

These were the Reagan years. Most people in the town where I had grown up referred to communism in daily conversation, right alongside talk of droughts and price ceilings and all the other evils of the world over which they had no control. Still, even within the parameters of our small town, my parents' fears felt different. They saw communism lurking everywhere, behind everything that was new to them or unfamiliar, behind everything that I had gone off to college and found myself drawn to: philosophy, feminism, poetry, my professors—even the Peace Corps, as I had discovered when I mentioned that I was thinking about applying, a revelation that made my mother cry. I had first noticed this difference in the sixth grade, when four of my classmates showed up at our door on Halloween with UNICEF boxes, requesting contributions to help poor children. "You can have candy or nothing," my mother told them, explaining, "We don't support communists in this house." She held out a Babe Ruth bar, gauging whether they were beyond salvation. They were.

That year, we had been presented with a new teacher, Mrs. Keller, who was not from our town, which meant that she was an outsider, and this meant that I paid a good deal of attention to everything she said and did. Early in the year, on a rainy afternoon when we were all feeling restless, Mrs. Keller had tried to teach us levitation, which we enjoyed so much that some of us went home and reported about our fun to our parents. I did not, for though I was just eleven, I sensed that levitation would be regarded with suspicion by my parents. Nonetheless, word came quickly back to the principal that we had been practicing levitation, which, it was understood, was a form of witchcraft and thus satanic.

We knew that Mrs. Keller had been spoken to, and for days we sat quietly in our seats, too ashamed to lift our eyes, but gently she wooed us back. Then, several weeks later, she played a scratchy recording of Poe's "The Tell-Tale Heart," which terrified us, and which we loved and begged to hear again, but which, it turned out, was also satanic, and again she was reprimanded. We watched as the joy that she took in teaching us dwindled, her spontaneity replaced with uncertainty, which spread to us so that we began to believe that we must say nothing of the excitement we felt in her classroom, as though excitement itself were suspect.

The day after Halloween, I sat at my desk and watched the four girls who had come to our door turn in their UNICEF boxes to Mrs. Keller and report, shyly, what my mother had said, how she had begged them to accept a candy bar and called them communists. Mrs. Keller started to say something but caught herself, her initial response giving way to a few bland comments about the good deed that the girls had done. Then, at the end of the school year, Mrs. Keller packed up her carefully decorated room—the maps of the world, the recordings of jazz and poetry, the pictures of her daughter, of whom we were all just a little jealous—and moved on.

When Marvin Helgarson asked us to introduce ourselves that first night, I said only that I was a Humanities major, one semester away from graduation. The Humanities department had recently declared a slogan—*Confronting the Ultimate Reality*—to explain what it was that we did in the Humanities, for apparently there was some confusion. I had found that we mainly spent a lot of time reading and talking about concepts that required capitalization—Beauty and Love, Suffering and Death, Guilt and Art. We also wrote papers about them, and often my professors wrote "interesting" or "hmm" next to my points, but they never wrote "correct." This was starting to feel stressful. It was like playing Find the Button, with people calling out, "You're getting warm!" every once in a while, but no matter how long you played, you never actually found the button.

Because there wasn't really a button. I got that. I understood that the Ultimate Reality was nebulous. Still, I was one semester away from graduation, and I knew that The Ultimate Reality was not something that you talked about at job interviews, to employers who wanted to know what relevant skills you had acquired over the last four years. Moreover, when I looked around at other students, they were learning how to generate spreadsheets and teach children to read, concrete, practical knowledge of the sort that you imagined people going to work and using, while I was becoming less equipped for the world with each passing day.

To make matters worse, when I visited my parents, which I did infrequently though they lived just an hour and fifteen minutes away, they always asked about my job prospects, sometimes while I was still getting out of the car. "What you want is to look for a company that'll keep you until you're ready to retire," my father said the last time I visited, and I said, "Why not just kill me now."

This was the sort of comment that made no sense to my parents, that made them think I had gone off to college and gotten myself hooked up with communists. Most nights, I lay in bed awake, imagining myself jobless and forced to move back into my parents' house, where we would sit at the dinner table eating overcooked pork chops and potatoes from my father's garden while they pointed out again and again that they were not surprised by my inability to find a job because nobody they knew had ever heard of such a thing as Humanities.

Tabatha and the crazy lady argued about "three fingers going" until Marvin said that it was a good time for a break. Usually, I stayed in the room during breaks, reviewing the next story up for discussion, but that night I went into the hallway and stood around with the others. I had trouble getting my structure straight before I started writing, and Marvin said that the problem might be that I did not figure out the *emotional thrust* of my stories early enough, which was probably true because, overall, I found *emotional thrust* an elusive concept, but I can see now that before I explain why I went out in the hallway, I need to explain about Clem.

The easiest way to begin is to say that Clem and I were friends, though, in retrospect, this seems dishonest because Clem annoyed me much more than he amused me, which is not to say that he couldn't be funny, but this story will mainly deal with annoyance because annoyance was the salient feature of our friendship. Our friendship began because Clem was crippled—"crippled" was his word, the one he insisted on—though not actually *because* he was crippled but because he blamed everything, including the fact that he had no friends, on being crippled. I befriended him primarily to prove him wrong about people, though it's clear now that Clem knew all along that that's what I was doing, which just proves that he was a very lonely person. I've always been intrigued by people like that, people who are mean and hate everyone and do everything they can to repel others—and then feel lonely about it.

Clem was mainly crippled on the left side; when he walked, he held his right arm aloft like the Statue of Liberty and pulled the rest of his body toward it. He told me that before the accident he was athletic but shy, that he gravitated toward solitary sports like golf and running. He was jogging when the accident happened, the morning after his high school graduation. The car that hit him kept going, so he lay by the road for over twenty minutes until a truck driver spotted him. He found out months later, after he came out of his coma, that the car had contained four of his classmates, all of whom had been too drunk to realize that they had even hit someone.

The accident turned Clem into a completely different person. He told me this one night as we looked through his senior yearbook, and I wondered (though did not ask) whether he remembered being that other person. I assumed that he did not, for it seemed to me that if he did remember, he would still *be* him.

"Do you think I'm good looking?" he would ask after a few beers, a question that I refused to answer because I saw it as a trap, saw that either answer would confirm what he already felt about people, which was that we were cruel, insincere, and stupid. The truth was that the accident had left him disfigured, though except for some scarring on his face, which he partially concealed with a black beard and sideburns, disfigured in a way that was not so much startling as simply ugly. Also, at times, his tongue appeared too big for his mouth and lolled outside. He looked like someone parents would instinctively move their children away from.

His brain had been damaged in a way that caused him to perceive everything as upside down and backward, so that what he saw as a 6 was really a 9. Over the years he adjusted by learning to write so that the words appeared upside down and backward to *him*, a process that was slow and messy. The college provided some assistance in the form of students who typed for him, but most tired of him quickly because he mainly dictated things that were pornographic, like the first story that he wrote for class about a cow named Bessie who had large udders but also a penis. He called the story "Bessie the Hermaphrodite Cow, No Bull," and nothing really happened in the story except that Bessie had sex nonstop with both bulls and cows. When it came time to critique the story, nobody said anything, not even the crazy lady, and finally Marvin did a line-by-line critique of the punctuation, which he said was "creative but at odds with the story."

In the year that Clem and I hung out together, I took him to doctor's appointments, shopped for his groceries, and listened to him rage. I drew the line at doing his homework, which he never did himself and which meant that he failed all of his classes and had been doing so, to the best of my knowledge, since he had enrolled in college three years earlier. His parents called me when they wanted to know how much money he had left or whether he was "keeping his spirits up" because they were afraid of him. I met them only once, on his birthday, when the four of us went to Mexican Village and he made his mother cry by announcing that she smelled like "crotch rot." She didn't, or at least I didn't smell anything, except tacos, which do have a yeasty corn smell.

Clem never missed an opportunity to suggest that he and I have sex, posing the question, always, in the most vulgar of terms. Thus, while Tabatha and the crazy lady argued that night about the gynecologist, he was hard at work on a picture of me and him as naked stick figures, which he labeled "Three Fingers Going." He slid it across the table toward me, and it took me a moment to understand the drawing, not only because it was poorly sketched but because it made no sense to me—there in a library, surrounded by books and people talking about words. As I ripped it up, Clem said, "Just so you know, before the accident, I wasn't into fat, ugly chicks." For the record, I wasn't really fat or ugly, but I wasn't exactly out of the woods when it came to fat and ugly either. Still, I knew that the sudden anger I felt had less to do with the words themselves than with the realization that I was sick of everything about Clem.

Out in the hallway, several of my classmates were standing around smoking and eating chocolate Easter eggs. Marvin once told us that we should use specific nouns, that instead of writing *candy*, we should say exactly what kind of candy—chocolate Easter eggs, for example—but he also told us to use details to establish time and setting, so I realize now that people are going to think that this happened at Easter, but it was actually several weeks after Easter and Melinda brought the eggs because she was tired of seeing them in her freezer. Nobody acted surprised that I was joining them in the hallway that night. Melinda offered me an egg, just as she did everyone else, and I stood next to her, unwrapping it and thinking about what to say.

"I liked your story about the drummer whose drum set falls out of the back of her truck," I told her.

She narrowed her eyes, not because of what I had said but because she was taking a drag from her cigarette. "Thanks," she said blowing out smoke.

Sometimes Melinda wore leather to class, so I asked her whether she had actually been in a band. "Sure," she said, as though I should know that the story was about her.

"Why'd you stop?" I asked.

"You read the story," she said.

"Couldn't you have bought new drums?"

"Well, yeah," she said. "But that's not really the point."

I nodded, but I didn't really know what the point was. Finally, I said, "I'm sorry, but what is the point?"

She smoked for a moment, and I felt better because it seemed then that maybe she was not sure of the point either. This was one of the advantages of smoking. It gave you the chance to think about what to say next without making it obvious that that's what you were doing. "I guess the point is that sometimes you reach a place in your life where you just want things to add up at the end of the day." She took another drag. "Do you know what I do now?" she asked.

"No," I said, worried that she had mentioned this during introductions the first night.

"I keep the books for the beet plant. Every night before I go home, I close out the books for the day, and I make sure that everything adds up. If something doesn't add up, I stay until it does. It's very gratifying—to go home each day knowing that everything has added up."

I nodded because I understood how this would be gratifying. In high school, I had been enamored of math and it had shocked everyone, friends and teachers and family, when I declared my intention to major in something else entirely, something that involved "reading and the world," which was how I had phrased it because I had not known how to explain what I was after any other way. Math came easily to me, too easily, and in my romanticized view of the world, this had struck me as a problem.

Around this time, the results of a battery of aptitude tests to which I had submitted began rolling in, all bearing the same news: that I was destined to become an engineer or a statistician or an accountant, careers in which things were meant to add up. I soon stopped showing these results to my parents, who were already bewildered by my announcement and could not imagine reading as an end in itself or what sort of living this would provide, but eventually, the results, each new one mirroring the others, had begun to worry me also, for I thought highly of tests, believing them almost infallible. Finally, one of them dealt a wild card, concluding that I was uniquely suited to be a forest ranger, no doubt because I had responded agreeably to questions about solitude and working alone. Still, this came as a great relief because there were few things that interested me less than nature, which meant that the tests had no more insight into me—or my future—than I did.

I had found myself missing math terribly that last year of college: the ease with which things added up, the logic and asymmetrical beauty of the equations, the straightforwardness of the signs and symbols, unequivocally urging me to add or subtract or divide. Of course, I did not say any of this to Melinda that night. I nodded, she finished her cigarette, and we went back into the classroom.

But I had a secret. I was taking calculus. Nobody knew, not my parents, who would have felt vindicated, or my Humanities friends, who would have seen it as a betrayal. The professor, Dr. Dillard, was a thin man in his forties with a habit of thrusting the chalk into his ear and twirling it nervously, only to become flustered when it no longer worked on the board. He regarded students as his natural enemies, and when we asked questions, which we did often since his explanations lacked clarity, he prefaced his equally hazy clarifications with the words: "Am I teaching complete and utter imbeciles?" We dealt with this the way that students generally deal with such things. We hated him.

Thus, when he arrived with his zipper open one morning several weeks into the term, nobody said a thing. We let him stand up there at the board, writing out equations and delivering his incomprehensible explanations with his fly not just undone but gaping like a hungry mouth. We did not laugh, but probably most of us took some pleasure in the situation, and finally an older man from Togo raised his hand and said in a kind, almost apologetic voice, "Excuse me, Doctor, but your zipper is not closed." He had a French accent and a low, buttery voice, which made even the word "zipper" sound exotic. Dr. Dillard asked the man to repeat what he had said because he had trouble understanding the man's accent. Actually, what he said was "I can't understand a damn word you're saying," and the man from Togo repeated it, enunciating and speaking more slowly but sounding just as kind and sensuous as the first time. It was clear that Dr. Dillard did understand then, for he turned quickly around and stared at the equation that he had been working out for us on the board, stared at it while we stared at him. He did not speak or reach down to fix his fly or attempt in any way to move the situation along, so after ten or fifteen minutes of terrible silence, we understood that class was over, and though we all hated him, I believe that, in that moment, we felt sorry for him, sorry for how small and hunched he seemed, for the way that he stood with his back to us, staring at an equation that had lost its meaning.

Dr. Dillard arrived for the next class with his zipper up. He stood at the front of the room facing us and announced that we would begin with a quiz, which we all failed because the quiz was over material that we were supposed to have covered during the last period. When he handed the quizzes back to us after the break, he did so in a frenetic, almost jaunty way—running up and down the aisles and announcing our grades, *zero zero zero*, loudly before tossing the quizzes down in front of us—and I realized then that even in math, things didn't always add up. Sometimes, there was just one side trying to be greater than the other.

After class that night, Clem acted as though I were going to drive him home as usual and then sit around watching him get drunk while listening to him explain that the world was made up of assholes, but when he started lurching after me, I turned and yelled, "Find your own way home," and then I walked away fast while he shouted after me that I hated cripples. He knew that I hated that kind of thing: screaming and public arguments and having strangers look at me, look at me and think that it must be true that I hated cripples because there I was, running away from one. Instead of going home, I went to Jack's, which I had been avoiding because of something that had happened there a couple of weeks earlier, and though it was probably just an anecdote, it was an anecdote that nearly broke my heart. It had to do with this old man who spent every night at Jack's, doing the splits for anyone who would buy him a drink, which, it turned out, was a lot of people. After I watched him do the splits seven times in two hours—and drink seven drinks in those same two hours—I went over and asked him how old he was.

"I'm seventy-six," he said, holding his hand up and wiggling the thumb and index finger, as though seventy-six were an age that could still be conveyed with fingers.

"Wow," I said unconvincingly. "You must be in very good health." I did not really know how to talk to old people.

"Yes," he said proudly. "I'm in perfect health," and then he proceeded to tell me a long story about how he had been diagnosed with a bad liver just six months earlier. He imitated his doctor telling him, "You've got to give up the booze," and then he told me, with a wheezy chuckle that made his nose squirt, that he had not given up *the booze* because he liked *the booze*. Instead, he had prayed about his liver before he went to bed one night, and during the night God came and performed surgery on him, actually fixed his liver while he was asleep.

"But how did you know that God operated on you?" I asked because how would you know such a thing.

"I'll tell you," he said triumphantly. "I knew it clear as cake cause when I woke up there was blood in my long johns, and I'll tell you what else—I got right out of bed and did ten pushups. I had the energy of a horse." He neighed, which made his nose squirt some more.

Honestly, I did not want to hear about the blood in his long johns because hearing about it made me picture it and picturing it made me queasy, especially on top of his squirting nose, but I thought about how lonely he must be to tell such a thing to a stranger. I bought two pickled eggs because that was the only food available at that time of night, and we sat at the bar to eat them, his teeth clacking as he chewed. I wanted to ask him about the expression he had used, "clear as cake," which I had never heard before, but I didn't because I suspected that "clear as cake" was something left over from an earlier life.

Two boys came over then with a shot of vodka, and he nearly fell off of his stool following them. I did not want to watch him do the splits again, especially now when all I would be thinking about was the blood in his long johns, so I left, but from outside, I could still hear the laughter and clapping that meant he had made it down to the floor again.

When I got to Jack's, I sat at the bar and ordered a beer and tried not to feel bad about running away from Clem. The bartender who had dished up the pickled eggs that night came down to where I was sitting and said, "Did you hear about Elmer? Died last night in his sleep."

"Who's Elmer?" I asked.

"Old guy that does the splits," he said. "Elmer."

"Oh," I said. "I know Elmer."

Some Humanities friends waved from a booth for me to join them. "Elmer died," I said as I sat down, and they said, "Who's Elmer?" just the way I had a few minutes earlier. "He's that old man who always did the splits," I said just the way the bartender had because when it came down to it, that's how everyone knew Elmer. For most people, doing the splits was Elmer's salient feature.

"Well, he was old," said one of my friends and the others nodded.

I don't know why this made me angry. It wasn't that I didn't think Elmer was old. He *was* old. I guess I just felt that what they were saying was that dying didn't mean anything when you were old. I wanted to tell them about how Elmer believed that God had operated on him in his sleep, about the blood in his long johns and how he said "clear as cake" because he'd once had a family, people who all sat around saying "clear as cake" without ever having to explain themselves because "clear as cake" meant something to them. I wanted them to understand that he wasn't just some old guy who did the splits for college students.

Instead, I went home and wrote my final story for Marvin Helgarson's class. In the story, an old man named Elmer does the splits—which I tried, unsuccessfully, to change to chin ups and then cartwheels—in an unnamed bar popular with college students who buy him drinks. Agatha, the main character, is majoring in math, and she saves Elmer by realizing that he has amnesia. She finds his family, who, it turns out, has been looking for him for three years, and when she calls them, she knows she has the right family because when Elmer's son describes the day that his father disappeared, he says, "I remember that day as clear as cake." In the final scene, Agatha drives Elmer to his family's house, even though he doesn't really want to go. This takes most of the day, and when she gets back to campus for her math class, the professor gives a pop quiz, which she aces even though she did not have time to study because of driving Elmer home. The story ended like this: "Agatha felt the knowledge taking shape inside of her, becoming a part of her, and then spilling onto the page, everything adding up."

When we discussed the story on the last night of class, Tabatha immediately raised her hand. "First of all," she said, "amnesia's such a cop out." She looked at me as though I had offended her in some very personal way.

"Okay," Marvin said. "Can you explain what you mean by 'cop out'?"

I did not really want her to explain, but she said, "It's such a cliché. Plus, Elmer's just some old guy who's going to be dead any day, so it really has to be Agatha's story."

"And you don't think it's her story now?" Marvin asked.

"It is, I guess. I just don't like her." She turned to me and said, "Maybe your life is like this, but nobody wants to read a story about some goody-two-shoes who always knows what to do. I think the story would be better if Agatha drinks too much because *she* doesn't know how to help Elmer, and the next morning *she* wakes up, and *she* doesn't remember anything."

"So she should just sit there having a good time while Elmer does the splits until he dies?" I said, even though we were not supposed to talk during our session.

"Okay," Marvin said. "What else?"

"I like the sex stuff," said Clem. We had not spoken since I ran away from him the week before.

"What sex stuff?" I said.

"When she's thinking about the blood in his long johns," Clem said.

Marvin jumped in then, asking what the story was about, and someone said, "It's about aging, I guess," and Marvin said, "Is it?," the way that teachers do to keep the discussion going. Someone else said that it was about age versus youth, or maybe hope or knowledge, and when Marvin asked me what I thought it was about, I said, "I don't know. I guess it's about compassion," and Tabatha looked at me as though I'd said it was about chewing gum.

"There's no compassion," she said. "She just pities him. They're not the same."

"Go on," said Marvin, but she shrugged as though there were nothing more to say.

"She just wants to feel good about herself," Clem said, surprising everyone, I think, because he generally restricted himself to making lewd comments. I knew that by "she," he meant me and that Marvin Helgarson maybe knew this also because he did not ask Clem to explain. Instead, Marvin said that class was over.

That was the last time I saw Clem, though I think about him from time to time. I picture him sitting in Marvin's class semester after semester, another student, always a woman, shuttling him home afterward, watching him drink and failing him in the same way that I did because I understand now that the kindest thing I could have done was to tell Clem what he already knew: that I would not have sex with him because he repulsed me, that I didn't even like him.

I got a B- in Marvin Helgarson's class, which didn't surprise me because I knew by then that I had no business being a writer. In his final comments, Marvin Helgarson said that my main problem was that I was actually *too good* a student, that I had followed every one of the rules and, in the process, I had *suffocated* my story, which was the way it worked in writing. I ended my stories as though it were the reader's birthday and I had tied everything up in a bow and handed it to the reader like a present. Readers, he said, liked to figure things out for themselves, but it seemed to me that if someone had read the whole story, they would want to know how things turned out: that I did not move in with my parents or join the Peace Corps, that I moved instead to New Mexico, where my plan was to forget about the Ultimate Reality and go back to studying math, that I somehow imagined this would be easy and everything would start adding up. But it was like Marvin Helgarson said: sometimes, you thought you knew what your character wanted and then you got to the end of your story and realized that you didn't understand this character you had created at all.

IMPASSE TEMPÊTE

BY BEN FOUNTAIN

2018 SIMPSON PRIZE FINALIST

He'd lived in Port-au-Prince his whole life. When I first knew him he liked to mock the Macoutes and their country ways, their bumbling attempts at urban cool. "Macoute guy, he dance like this," Pierre would say, stomping and lurching around like a man trying to fling a crab off his foot. "But you born in Port-au-Prince, you from the city, you dance like this," and he'd ease into a fluid shuffle and glide that made you thankful for your eyes. But that was years ago, and now he never left his house except to see the doctor. One of his legs was always numb, and high blood pressure made him dizzy, and with his cataracts he felt lost on the street.

"I can see far," he told me, "I can see the mountains, but I can't see your face. Your face just look all dusty to me."

People kept wandering through the room where we sat, his wife, kids and grandkids, nieces and nephews, neighborhood kids. It wasn't a big house, four cinderblock rooms next to the massive gulch that cut through Martissant. When he'd first shown me where he planned to build his house, this part of Martissant looked like a demolition site, a no man's land of scorched rubble and used-up dirt. But a bidonville had grown up around Pierre's house, and the unpaved alley that led through the neighborhood had an official name now, Impasse Tempête.

I can see the mountains, but I can't see your face. He brought out a plastic shopping bag filled with medicines and described each one for me, going by feel, recognizing them by the shapes of the bottles. Yesterday's storm had almost flooded his house, a spectacular *lavalas* that roared down the mountains and overflowed the gulch, spilling into the antheap network of alleys and paths. *Nou la,* Pierre said when I asked about the storm. *Grâce à Dieu, nou la anko.* We're here. Thanks to God, we're still here. The gulch held five or six feet of standing water today, a thick, sludgy roux that roiled here and there with jets of methane gas bubbling up from below. From the look of the sky there would be no storms today, only the sun beating down like punishment.

We sat in the soft gray light of the room, sweating and drinking warm 7-Up. As always, he wanted to talk politics, although his mind kept wandering, shuffling past and present like a deck of cards.

"You see Aristide up there?" he asked, pointing at the ceiling.

"He's sort of hard to miss." Whenever that big black helicopter screamed across the sky, the entire city knew their president was on the move. Aristide in his helicopter, far above us all; that story had turned bitter a long time ago, and as we talked Pierre seemed to get the priest and Papa Doc confused in his mind. But soon he came back to the present.

"That thing in Iraq," he said, "everybody in Haiti know what it's about. They only want the oil."

I nodded. "You guys are way ahead of us Americans."

"Mohammad Atta, you know that guy? He marry a Haitian girl."

"I didn't know that."

"CIA all over Haiti looking for that girl, they take her away. Take her to Cuba, people say. Nobody see that girl again." He took a drink of 7-Up and shook his head, faking a long look at me. "That guy Bush," he asked, his voice cracking with a plaintive, wondering note, "what does he *want?*"

A fair question. "Like you said, Pierre, I think he wants the oil. And whatever else Cheney tells him to want."

Pierre smiled, looked down at his hands. He knew how it worked, he had a veteran's highly developed feel for the personal aspects of blood politics, the vast range of psychoses and ecstatic delusions from which the grand-scale mischiefs spring. He'd spent his life on the receiving end of such things, and here in his cinderblock house, next to that latrine of a gulch, he could smell the sickness from three thousand miles away.

I'd brought a few gifts—some scarves for his wife, a boom box for the kids, a fancy silk shirt for Pierre himself. "Next birthday I have sixty years, " he said after I handed out the gifts. "I make sixty, then I finish."

"Oh Pierre, don't talk like that."

But he shook his head. "I work too hard when I was young, I hurt my body. Now," he paused, trying to find me through the haze of his milky eyes, "I make sixty, then I finish."

I argued, but suspected he was right; in fifteen years I'd never heard him speak a false or foolish word. There's something surreal about seeing an old friend when we know it's for the last time, a shameful gap between the reality right before our eyes and the kinds of facts our minds can absorb. I'd come here fifteen years ago wanting to learn the country, hoping to understand something of how the world works, and had met Pierre on that first trip. He'd been my keeper, tutor, and guide ever since, going along on all my trips into the boonies and slums, never complaining, talking us out of tight spots, patiently schooling me in the business of life in this place. To say he was the Virgil to my Dante would be stretching it—just a little—and yet he did show me something of hell, and where to look for grace and mercy in the midst of it.

If he ever thought badly of me for needing something from Haiti, this place where so many people already needed so much, he never let it show. He gave me permission to keep coming, and in my own way, the American way, with money, I tried to keep some semblance of balance in the exchange. This last visit was part of what was owed from my side; it was a stiff, awkward hour for both of us, but necessary, or so it seemed to me. When I left, he insisted on walking me to the car, and so we made our way down the path with Pierre dragging his bum leg, one hand on my arm, the other propped on the shoulder of his oldest grandson. Where the path intersected Impasse Tempête, we stopped, and he solemnly accepted an embrace from me.

"Only God know everything you do for me," he murmured, clutching my arm, strangely desperate to speak this last piece of news. "Only *God*, and *me*."

He and his grandson stood on the path as I made my way to the car. Some children were gathered on the steps of a nearby doorway; a girl of ten or eleven was sitting among them, leaning over a plastic bucket between her legs. In her hands she held a bird of some kind, a dove or small chicken, and she was plucking the animal alive, shredding clumps of bloody feathers into the bucket. I had to look twice to understand what I was seeing, this glistening liverish thing jerking and twitching in the girl's hands, and then I couldn't stop looking. She was almost finished, stripping the last downy patches off the bird's back, its delicate black eyes bright with shock. I suppose that humankind's most enduring hope is for the suffering here on earth to serve some purpose; we have to hope, otherwise we'd all go crazy, but the sight of that miserable bird just disgusted me. I scolded the girl in my bad Creole, then turned to Pierre to share my disgust, to have my fit of revulsion confirmed. I think I wanted him to scold the girl too, but Pierre hadn't noticed our little scene. He'd lifted his head and was looking beyond us, past the intricate sprawl and warp of his ruined neighborhood, his pale eyes searching the distance for what might be left of this world to see.

"A WOUNDED DEER—LEAPS HIGHEST": MOTIVES FOR METAPHOR

BY JOYCE CAROL OATES

SIMPSON PROJECT/LAFAYETTE LIBRARY
WRITER-IN-RESIDENCE

*DELIVERED AT THE LAFAYETTE PUBLIC LIBRARY
MARCH 2018*

Many of you are familiar with the thesis of *The Wound and the Bow: Seven Studies in Literature* (1941)—Edmund Wilson's highly influential examination of the works of Sophocles, Casanova, Dickens, Kipling, Wharton, Hemingway, and Joyce as the works relate to their lives. In Wilson's theory of the genesis of art it is argued that the artist is one who has suffered a mysterious wound, a wound that "never heals," and that art is a response to this wound, a compensatory strategy, in effect a kind of fierce and protracted denial of the primal wound— the wound that "never heals." Recall Freud's succinct, rather cynical description of the artist and his craft: "Art hallucinates ego-mastery."

Ironically, art can "hallucinate" a kind of mastery even when the art is, like Samuel Beckett's great work, almost entirely about disintegration and loss of control, that is, a loss of "mastery." To gain control of loss one must catalogue loss—one must give it a name, a form, a meaning. Many of us gathered here can chant together the low-keyed yet thrilling opening lines of Elizabeth Bishop's "One Art":

> The art of losing isn't hard to master;
> So many things seem filled with the intent
> To be lost that their loss is no disaster.

Emily Dickinson is our great artist of loss, oblique tragedy, unspeakable sorrow translated into unexpectedly vivid dramatic images:

A *Wounded* Deer—leaps highest—
I've heard the Hunter tell—
'Tis but the Extasy of *death*—
And then the Brake is still!

The *Smitten* Rock that gushes!
The *trampled* Steel that springs!
A Cheek is always redder
Just where the Hectic sings!

Mirth is the Mail of Anguish—
In which it Cautious Arm,
Lest anybody spy the blood
And "you're hurt" exclaim!

Through literary history, from Renaissance sonneteers who "sweated with heat"—yet were "freezing cold"—who "starved," "pined," and "thirsted"—(in the throes of love)—making of the intensity of their emotions the most exquisitely wrought verse, to contemporary writers who take as their task the recording of the most minuscule details of their lives, it has seemed that the quintessential artist feels more deeply than others, and is unusually sensitive; in much of Thomas Mann's work, notably the long, quasi-autobiographical "Tonio Kroger," the blond Germanic schoolboy Hans is "uncommonly handsome and well-built, broad in the shoulders...with keen, far-apart, steel-blue eyes" while Tonio Kroger, the budding artist, has "finely chiseled features" and "dark eyes, with delicate shadows and too heavy lids, [that] looked dreamily and a little timorously on the world." Tonio Kroger is a very young Aschenbach, of *Death in Venice*; over-sensitive, over-emotional, thus obliged to suppress his emotions, Tonio stands at a distance from the world of his adolescent contemporaries. Tonio's "dark, fiery" mother is a Southern European; Tonio's father is a repressed Northern European businessman—of course, a financial success. Out of Tonio's unarticulated love for Hans, that's to say the artist's love for "authentic/ unexamined life," is born the artist's art, in this case a much-admired literary art that becomes in time "fastidious, precious, morbidly sensitive...,[offended by] the banal." How many times we find reiterated in art of the late nineteenth and early twentieth century the paradox that fascinated Mann, that "he who lives does not [create]; that one must die to life in order to be utterly a creator." Slyly Mann speaks of those persons—(his own kind?)—"to whom poetry serves as a sort of mild revenge upon life."

It's the impassioned cry of self-reproach of Flaubert, speaking of a wife and mother surrounded by her children—"Ils sont dans le vrai." The sentiment is reiterated by Kafka with yet more despairing self-loathing—the distance between the (hunger) artist and those who dwell, unthinkingly, in "le vrai"—the so-called truth of domestic felicity.

We are inclined in our time to dismiss the broad cultural, ethnic, and psychological stereotypes that so impressed Thomas Mann; we distrust the condescension that informs the "envy" of a man of great talent for the wife and mother—the "female"—whose abode is domestic life.

To claim that the "wounded" artist is (probably) more sensitive than other people may be a false claim: is Stephen Dedalus more sensitive, more nuanced in his emotions, than Leopold Bloom? Faulkner's Benjy, of *The Sound and the Fury*, wholly lacking speech, may be the most sensitive of all the Compsons. It is entirely possible that non-artists are as sensitive as artists but lack the resources, the talent, the time, the energy and the desire to express their sensitivities as artists do; that is, to labor to create products that require effort, craft, vision and cunning, and the leisure for these, which is not so common in history. Who can say but that enslaved persons and indentured servants were not among the most sensitive inhabitants of the North American continent but were forbidden to express their visions; who can say but that entire cultures existed before the settling of the continent, that were eradicated by the conqueror, or in the ways of acquisition dismissed as of no aesthetic or moral worth; who knows but that the illiterate are not in fact often more eloquent than literate but have lacked the means to express their eloquence; as Virginia Woolf asked, what of Shakespeare's sister? Why have we not heard of *her*?

We all know why we have not heard of Shakespeare's sister, let alone read something by her. And by countless others who have been oppressed, their voices muffled, extinguished.

◆◆◆

"I have been one acquainted with the night," Frost says in his beautifully nuanced sonnet. "I have outwalked the furthest city lights." In a dream landscape of self-recrimination where "the time was neither wrong nor right."

No one has ever lived who has not been in some significant way "wounded." Eventually, life "wounds" us in the simple living of it: those we'd believed to be permanent around us, a fixed and reliable audience to our smallest dramas, begin to fall away, vanish. How chilling to realize as a child that you are not at the very center of others' concern—how chilling, as an adult, to realize that your love for others will not be enough to save them. Yet, most people don't cultivate an art to compensate for woundedness: obviously there is something special, something "extra," about the individual who is to become an artist, otherwise everyone would be an artist. The fallacy is to think that art is *only* a consequence of woundedness, or, to use a more clinical term, neurosis; or, indeed, that art has any essential relationship at all with woundedness. It's as likely that art is a sustained and cultivated expression of the child's enormous capacity for playful creation, fantasizing, and storytelling. Here is the true wellspring of art: sheer astonishing energy.

Yet there are those who find themselves deeply moved by the woundedness of others, which may be more extreme than their own, and more worthy of attention. If art is, in some essential way, a mirror held up to its time, it is also a distorting mirror; it is not a merely reflective mirror; it does not care to present what (merely) *is*. Perhaps it is a worthier challenge to tell the stories of others, our neighbors, with as much care as if they were our own, a variant on the most elemental of ethical injunctions: Do unto others as you would they would do unto you. Which is to suggest that the expression of "woundedness" may not be traced back exclusively to personal experience; you might, if you are sympathetic, if you have a natural concern for others, have only to glance up from your own life, out of your own experience, to see that there are others, many others, who have not your advantages, perhaps, and might require you to speak for them, or to aid in their speaking for themselves, and in so doing call attention to them; if they cannot tell their own stories it is possible, though it is not required, that you might tell their stories. Perhaps in the end it is the powerful story that must be told, that is embodied in a singular work, *Frankenstein; or, the Modern Prometheus,* for instance, or *Uncle Tom's Cabin*; and the identity of the storyteller or storytellers not so significant.

I speak as one who was not romantically "wounded" into art but rather looked up from my life, from the protective aura of my family, and saw in the near vicinity of our family farm (in western New York State, in the 1940s and 1950s), the lives of children my age, and the lives of their families—astonishing stories of pain and loss, protracted privation, hardship, that would have defeated me; yet these children, or most of them, persevered, like my own parents, who lived through the Depression, maintaining what I recall as the most remarkable optimism and a total lack of self-pity. How ironic, these Americans who'd had virtually no schooling, who'd had to drop out of even rural schools by the age of twelve, embodied the "self-reliance" of which Emerson spoke from a position of privileged authority. That vanishing, or vanished America!

What galvanizes some of us into art isn't *This is my story* but *How is this not my story.*

"Bearing witness" is very possibly the most inspiring of literary motives once one has moved past the boundless energies of sheer creativity of childhood. Allowing others to see what should be seen, what should not be allowed to vanish; the lives of our ancestors for instance who were, in their time, immigrants coming to America often under terrible conditions, in a time before social welfare of any kind, when public amenities were few, and nothing could be taken for granted. This is the great drama of America: immigrant succession, assimilation. When I first began school in the early 1940s there were no school buses—at least not in the wilds of rural western New York State. You walked to a one-room school a mile or two miles in devastating winter winds and snowstorms—or you didn't. No one would much care, no one would miss you. But by the time I entered sixth grade there was bus service, to carry me to school in a small city seven miles away; buses would carry me to schools for the remainder of my public school education, and this public education allowed me, in time, to make my way into a very different America, and eventually here—to this very podium. In this American New Dark Age of meanness and privation, in which tax money for public amenities has been routed into bloated military budgets, and the very concept of "public amenities" is under attack, it is good to recall that nothing can be taken for granted; no vigilance on our parts is excessive, in protecting our hard-won democratic institutions.

"Bearing witness" means giving voice to those whose voices have been muted, or destroyed; those who have been victims; those whose stories require a larger audience than they have received. The boldest act of bearing witness in our literature is surely Harriet Beecher Stowe's *Uncle Tom's Cabin*—an astonishing imaginative achievement in the form of a melodramatic fiction exposing the horrors of slavery to a mass-market readership at a time when the teachings and preachings of Abolitionism were reaching an impassioned but limited audience. And thinking of Stowe's radical appropriation of lives very different from her own makes me think of Eudora Welty's memorable short story "Where Is the Voice Coming From?" (1963)—an exquisite miniature in which Welty dares to take on the voice of a white racist Mississippian who murders a black man in circumstances approximating the murder of NAACP field secretary Medgar Evers in June 1963, in Welty's hometown of Jackson. Two white women writers, of what might be called a genteel class—stirred to moral indignation by the horrors of history erupting about them.

The wish to move others to a course of action through sympathy, evoked in a reportorial manner—this is the basis for political, propaganda-art, but these are works of art that transcend their circumstances. Most of the great novels of Dickens, but particularly *Hard Times* and *Oliver Twist*; Stephen Crane's early, crudely effective *Maggie: A Girl of the Streets*; Upton Sinclair's *The Jungle,* the first and most renowned of nearly one hundred books by Sinclair, a devout lifelong Socialist. Frank Norris's *McTeague* and *The Octopus* are savage critiques of rapacious American capitalism; "class war" might be identified as the basis of such novels as Theodore Dreiser's *Sister Carrie* and *An American Tragedy* and of John Dos Passos's enormously influential *USA;* the failure of American society to live up to its democratic ideals in such works of fiction as Sinclair Lewis's *Main Street* and *Babbitt*, John Steinbeck's *The Grapes of Wrath, East of Eden,* and *Of Mice and Men*, and that most astonishing of visionary / revolutionary novels, from a perspective until the time of its publication (1940) virtually unknown to American readers, Richard Wright's *Native Son*—a Dostoyevskian descent into the abyss of northern urban racist America that refuses to indulge its readers with a "heroic" black protagonist whom they might champion like the "good Negroes" of *Uncle Tom's Cabin.*

Even in our post-Modern era, mainstream American literature with its predilection for liberal sympathies with the disenfranchised and impoverished, the great effort of the 19th and 20th century novel to draw attention to social injustice and inequality, remains the most attractive of literary traditions. In Toni Morrison's classic *Beloved,* for instance, slave narrative sources have been appropriated and refashioned into a highly stylized art both morally incensed and aesthetically ambitious. Our recently deceased, much missed colleague Edgar Doctorow began his career by reconstructing the lives of the "atom bomb spies" Ethel and Julius Rosenberg in *The Book of Daniel*; through the much-acclaimed *Ragtime, Loon Lake, World's Fair* and *The March* Doctorow appropriated for his subjects the volatile issues of class and race in America; Doctorow's more recent novels have been shaped by oral histories: "Every writer speaks for a community." Other writers whose work is suffused with a sense of social justice and a wish to dramatize the vagaries of American life with no diminution of art include our dear, late friend Robert Stone whose *Dog Soldiers, A Flag for Sunrise,* and *Damascus Gate* are among our great political novels; Russell Banks, whose sympathy for individuals both like, and radically unlike, himself has given us such extraordinary works of fiction as *Continental Drift, Cloudsplitter, The Darling,* and *Lost Memory of Skin;* John Edgar Wideman, whose fiction and memoirs constitute a scathing indictment of what Wideman has called "the American darkness"; Louise Erdrich, whose minutely chronicled, magic-realist interwoven tales of Native American lives in the northern Midwest constitute an achievement to set beside that of William Faulkner; and Susan Straight who, from the start of her career, has immersed herself in the lives of women and girls, families, in cultural crisis, in a series of works of fiction bearing intimate and unsparing witness to what one might call a politically marginalized America beset by problems of poverty, racial discrimination, and injustice.

In more recent years American writers have written boldly across divides of class, age, ethnic identity, and gender. Outstanding among these have been Anthony Marra, the much-acclaimed young author of *A Constellation of Vital Phenomena* and *The Tsar of Love and Techno,* set in Chechnya and the former USSR respectively; Viet Thanh Nguyen whose *The Sympathizer* employs an intricately self-reflexive Nabokovian literary style in which to present a portrait of a Vietnamese communist double-agent who survives the Fall of Saigon to relocate in an America fraught with questions of political and personal identity; Atticus Lish, whose *Preparations for the Next Life* is, in part, an extraordinary immersion into the interior life of a female Chinese "illegal immigrant" in New York City; Whitney Terrell, whose *The Good Lieutenant* explores the tragic complexities of the Iraqi War from the perspective of a young female Army lieutenant from the Midwest; T. Geronimo Johnson, whose *Welcome to Braggsville* is an extravagantly inventive, linguistically daring novel imagining the voice of a young white Berkeley undergraduate from the deepest of Deep South America; the Mexican-born Valeria Luiselli, whose tour de force assemblage of lyric, Borgesian tall tales, *The Story of My Teeth*, is a comic memoir of a Mexican estate auctioneer that defies the logic of conventional narrative and "characterization"; Jesmyn Ward, whose *Salvage the Bones* and *Sing, Unburied, Sing* are feats of lyricism set in rural Mississippi that give voice to individuals whose lives are lived at the margins of white America; and Dexter Palmer, whose *Version Control* is a perhaps the strangest fictional work of imagined voices and subjects, set in a surreal near-future, or several near-futures, as well as several pasts, in which issues of race play virtually no role at all, unless a mysterious and indefinable role.

◆◆◆

We must trust the human imagination—its predilection for digging at the roots of things, for prying at what is "fixed," for soaring boldly into the clouds. We must hesitate to suggest boundaries, perimeters. Let us strive to dissolve borders—in the words of Australian poet Thomas Kinsella, let us cultivate "international regionalism." Is it better to provide palliative answers, or to ask provocative questions? Is it better to carefully transcribe the close-at-hand, which can be safely confirmed, or to leap perilously into the unknown?

Should there be any restraints to the imagination? Boundaries, borders of "good taste"? We know that "good taste" may be a code phrase for "disturbing"—"unsettling"—as, in the example of women's writing, it was considered in some (male, conservative) quarters that the very subjects of female preoccupations—childbirth, child-rearing, domestic life—were considered vulgar, un-artistic. Should the audacious young poet Anne Sexton have been allowed to write so bluntly of sexual appetite, the experience of living in a physical (female) body, the "almost unspeakable" yearning for death (by suicide)? It was considered audacious—"offensive"—that the young German artist Anselm Kiefer dared to "reenact" the Nazi salute in his controversial "Occupations and Heroic Symbols" series in the 1960s and 1970s, calling Germany to task for its collective amnesia. "Obscene"—"offensive"—"in bad taste": photographers like Nan Goldin, Robert Mapplethorpe, Peter Hugar, Emmett Gowin, and Sally Mann have made of their most intimate relationships powerful/ controversial subjects for art, like novelists John Rechy, Hubert Selby, Jr., Edmund White and others for whom sexual identity is bound up with the worth of the spirit in defiance to authoritative normative heterosexuality/ conformity.

In an earlier era Kate Chopin dared to write of the inner, secretive, erotic lives of outwardly conventional women, usually married, and Christian; Chopin was made to pay dearly for her honesty, that's to say her refusal to be hypocritical about marriage and domestic life. William Faulkner exposed racist hypocrisy and pseudo-Christianity in the Old South, specifically Mississippi; in an astonishing sequence of novels (*As I Lay Dying, The Sound and the Fury, Absalom, Absalom!, Light in August, The Hamlet*) he dared to give voice to illiterate poor whites and Negroes in a highly stylized, experimental fiction that challenged the very foundations of realism. With similar boldness the Modernist Jean Toomer explored the sensual, instinctive, frequently tragic lives of black women and men of the rural South, in the unique prose-poem novel *Cane*. D.H. Lawrence dared to write openly, ecstatically about sexual experience, in violation of conventional norms of literature; James Joyce dared to put into prose fiction those bodily functions, those "taboo" words, those stray thoughts and impressions that constitute our mental lives, petty as well as heroic, that had never before been acknowledged in "serious" literature.

(Of course, both Lawrence and Joyce were subjected to the indignities of censure and censorship; Joyce's first book *Dubliners*, the least offensive of his books, was publicly burned in Ireland when the author was in his early twenties. "Ireland is the sow that devours her young"—as Joyce bitterly observed.)

As nature is said to abhor a vacuum, so the artist seems to abhor "taboo" even as she is fascinated by it—the dread sanctity of taboo. We are drawn to investigate what is forbidden to us. *You can't write about that!—you can't expect to make art out of that*—these warnings ring like invitations. Who could have predicted that one of the most brilliantly inventive depictions of racial relations in 21st century America would be an unclassifiable film marketed as a "horror comedy"—Jordan Peele's *Get Out*? Or that, within the same year, steadfast in its realist conventions as if it had been made fifty years ago, Dee Rees' beautiful and deeply moving *Mudbound*, which dares to end on a note of hope where a bleaker conclusion might have seemed inevitable. Who could predict that stand-up comics wielding wit with the savage indignation of a Diogenes or a Jonathan Swift would become the most acute of political commentators, pitching painful truths in an era badly needed to hear them?—or that such comic performances have increasingly come to seem like new, startlingly relevant art-forms or genres created by individuals for whom conventional forms of expression are too confining?

We applaud these innovations and encourage more. More risky undertakings in the name of "speaking truth to power"—or in the name of sheer comic excess. More experimentations with genre. More publishing projects that introduce readers to writers both emerging and established, from cultures distant from our own. Especially we crave radical and subversive art from the margins of society, that challenges the authority of the center. More quirky, stubborn, rebellious voices to counteract the ubiquitous drone of social-media culture. More public support for all the arts—visual, musical, theatrical, dance, print—and not just the arts that reflect our own convictions.

If our art sometimes provokes unexpected reactions this is the price we must pay for our commitment to bearing witness in a turbulent world.

◆◆◆

Yet, recall Milton's beautiful sonnet "On His Blindness" which ends with the line—"They also serve who only stand and waite…." There is an art that is not an activist art, and does not (conspicuously) bear witness to social and political conditions. There is an art that aspires to timelessness. There is an art that aspires to beauty—possibly, the beauty of pure forms. It may be a deeply personal art, that is yet universal. It may be oblique, indirect, subtle without being reclusive; an art that can be bold, even brazen, in its uniqueness, revealing its intransigent truths in ways that are not obviously political, or historical; the art of an Emily Dickinson, for instance, written in the very shadow of the Civil War, in contrast to the ebulliently outward, communal voice of her contemporary Walt Whitman, who wrote directly of the Civil War; an art that "tells all the Truth but tells it Slant—Success in Circuit lies." It may be the singular, subjective art of the "blue guitar" of Wallace Stevens's poem of 1937 "The Man With the Blue Guitar—

> They said, "You have a blue guitar.
> You do not play things as they are."
>
> The man replied, "Things as they are
> Are changed upon the blue guitar."

In this way the world is not captured, nor "reported upon," but—uniquely—mirrored. To write such a poem in 1937, at the height, or the depths, of the American Depression, was a bold stand of the poet, going against the grain of the era. It was Stevens who once allegedly stood up at a literary gathering to make the statement: "I've been asked to speak of the social obligation of the poet. He has none."

This provocatively patrician remark of Wallace Stevens is after all the essence of the artist, individual, stubborn, rebellious, unchartable and ungovernable: art for its own unique sake, and not for the sake of society. Art in the sake of individual vision, and not for the sake of effecting change in others. When Philip Guston radically changed his art, in the 1960s, turning from his transcendentally beautiful Abstract Expressionist canvases and creating intentionally ugly, banal, cartoon-like images (including hooded figures meant to evoke the Ku Klux Klan), most of the art world ostracized him; friends he'd known well for years ceased to speak to him; yet his friend and fellow artist William de Kooning assured him that he'd done the right thing, following his instinct—"We're not on a baseball team." In a time of crisis like the present, such quiet voices may speak as forcefully as loud voices. The "small, still voice" of which Doris Lessing spoke—(though Lessing was herself an activist, socially involved and visionary writer.) The poet in the tradition of William Carlos Williams, in which the dailyness of life is celebrated, and not its cataclysms; the poet in the tradition of Elizabeth Bishop, seeing in the near-at-hand something like the very cosmos. The subdued voice and not the vatic voice: the precision of language itself, which is a kind of devotion. "The sentence in itself beautiful"—as Virginia Woolf has said. Does an exquisitely wrought poem carry a resonance far beyond the most vehement opinion piece? Does an arrestingly original work of visual art, a work of surpassingly beautiful or problematic music, lodge more deeply in the soul than the most strident public art? The poet in the tradition of Czeslaw Miloz: "It seems that I was called for this: to glorify things just because they are."

The way of "bearing witness" and the way of the "blue guitar"— through a lifetime, we are likely to be both; and, urgently, we need both.

HAZARDS OF TIME TRAVEL

A NOVEL

BY JOYCE CAROL OATES

"Time travel"—and its hazards—are made literal as a recklessly idealistic girl dares to test the perimeters of her tightly controlled (future) world and is punished by being sent back in time to a region of North America— "Wainscotia, Wisconsin"—that existed eighty years before. Cast adrift in time in this idyllic Midwestern town she is set upon a course of "rehabilitation"—but cannot resist falling in love with a fellow exile and questioning the constraints of the Wainscotia world.

(AN EXCERPT)

"GOOD NEWS!"

Or so at first it seemed.

I'd been named valedictorian of my class at Pennsboro High School. And I'd been the only one at our school, of five students nominated, to be awarded a federally-funded Patriot Democracy Scholarship.

My mother came running to hug me, and congratulate me. And my father, though more warily.

"That's our girl! We are so proud of you."

The principal of our high school had telephoned my parents with the good news. It was rare for a phone to ring in our house for most messages came electronically and there was no choice about receiving them.

And my brother Roderick came to greet me with a strange expression in his face. He'd heard of Patriot Democracy Scholarships, Roddy said, but had never known anyone who'd gotten one. While he'd been at Pennsboro High he was sure that no one had ever been named a Patriot Scholar.

"Well. Congratulations, Addie."

"Thanks! I guess."

Roddy, who'd graduated from Pennsboro High three years before, and was now working as a barely paid intern in the Pennsboro branch of the NAS Media Dissemination Bureau (MDB), was grudgingly admiring. Smiling at me strangely—just his mouth, not his eyes. I thought— *He's jealous. He can't go to a real university.*

I never knew if I felt sorry for my hulking-tall brother who'd cultivated a wispy little sand-colored beard and mustache, and always wore the same dull-brown clothes, that were a sort of uniform for lower-division workers at MDB, or if—actually—I was afraid of him. Inside Roddy's smile there was a secret little smirk just for *me*.

When we were younger Roddy had often tormented me—"teasing" it was called (by Roddy). Both our parents worked ten-hour shifts and Roddy and I were home alone together much of the time. As Roddy was the older, it had been Roddy's task to *take care of your little sister*. What a joke! But a cruel joke, that doesn't make me smile.

Now we were older, and I was tall myself (for a girl of my age: five feet eight), Roddy didn't torment me quite as much. Mostly it was his expression—a sort of shifting, frowning, smirk-smiling, meant to convey that Roddy was thinking certain thoughts best kept secret.

That smirking little smile just for me—like an ice-sliver in the heart.

My parents had explained: it was difficult for Roddy, who hadn't done well enough in high school to merit a scholarship even to the local NAS state college, to see that I was doing much better than he'd done in the same school. Embarrassing to him to know that his younger sister earned higher grades than he had, from the very teachers he'd had at Pennsboro High. And Roddy had little chance of ever being admitted to a federally mandated four-year university, even if he took community college courses, and our parents could afford to send him.

Something had gone wrong during Roddy's last two years of high school. He'd become scared about things—maybe with reason. He'd never confided in me.

At Pennsboro High—as everywhere in our nation, I suppose—there was a fear of seeming "smart"—(which might be interpreted as "too smart")—which would result in calling unwanted attention to you. In a

True Democracy all individuals are *equal*—no one is *better than anyone else.* It was OK to get B's, and an occasional A-; but A's were risky, and A+ was very risky. In his effort not to get A's on exams, though he was intelligent enough, and had done well in middle school, Roddy seriously missed, and wound up with D's.

Dad had explained: it's like you're a champion archer. And you have to shoot to miss the bull's eye. And something willful in you assures that you don't just miss the bull's eye but the entire damned target.

Dad had laughed, shaking his head. Something like this had happened to him.

Poor Roddy. And poor Adriane, since Roddy took out his disappointment on me.

It wasn't talked about openly at school. But we all knew. Many of the smartest kids held back in order not to call attention to themselves. HSPSO (Home Security Public Safety Oversight) was reputed to keep lists of potential dissenters / MI's / SI's, and these were said to contain the names of students with high grades and high IQ scores. Especially suspicious were students who were good at science—these were believed to be too "questioning" and "skeptic" about the guidelines for curriculum at the school, so experiments were no longer part of our science courses, only just "science facts" to be memorized ("gravity causes objects to fall," "water boils at 212 degrees F.," "cancer is caused by negative thoughts," "the average female IQ is 7.55 points lower than the average male IQ, adjusting for ST status").

Of course it was just as much of a mistake to wind up with C's and D's—that meant that you were *dull-normal*, or it might mean that you'd deliberately sabotaged your high school career. Too obviously "holding back" was sometimes dangerous. After graduation you might wind up at a community college hoping to better yourself by taking courses and trying to transfer to a state school but the fact was, once you entered the work-force in a low-level category, like Roddy at MDB, you were there forever.

Nothing is ever forgotten, no one is going anywhere they aren't already at. This was a saying no one was supposed to say aloud.

So, Dad was stuck forever as an ME2—medical technician, second rank—at the district medical clinic where staff physicians routinely consulted him on medical matters, especially pediatric oncology—physicians whose salaries were five times Dad's salary.

Dad's health benefits, like Mom's, were so poor, Dad couldn't even get treatment at the clinic he worked in. We didn't want to think what it would mean if and when they needed serious medical treatment.

I hadn't been nearly as cautious in school as Roddy. I enjoyed school where I had (girl) friends close as sisters. I liked quizzes and tests—they were like games which, if you studied hard, and memorized what your teachers told you, you could do well.

But then, sometimes I tried harder than I needed to try.

Maybe it was risky. Some little spark of defiance provoked me.

But maybe also (some of us thought) school wasn't so risky for girls. There had been only a few DASTADs—Disciplinary Actions Securing Threats Against Democracy—taken against Pennsboro students in recent years, and these students had all been boys in category ST3 or below.

(The highest ST—SkinTone—category was 1: "Caucasian." Most residents of Pennsboro were ST1 or ST2 with a scattering of ST3's. There were ST4's in a neighboring district and of course dark-complected ST workers in all the districts. We knew they existed but most of us had never seen an actual ST10.)

It seems like the most pathetic vanity now, and foolishly naive, but at our school I was one of those students who'd displayed some talent for writing, and for art; I was a "fast study" (my teachers said, not entirely approvingly), and could memorize passages of prose easily. I did not believe that I was the "outstanding" student in my class. That could not be possible! I had to work hard to understand math and science, I had to read and reread my homework assignments, and to rehearse quizzes and tests, while to certain of my classmates these subjects came naturally. (ST2's and 3's were likely to be Asians, a minority in our district, and these girls and boys were very smart, yet not aggressive in putting themselves forward, that's to say *at risk*.) Yet somehow it happened that Adriane Strohl wound up with the highest grade-point average in the Class of '23—4.3 out of 5.

My close friend Paige Connor had been warned by her parents to hold back—so Paige's average was only 4.1. And one of the obviously smartest boys, whose father was MI, like my Dad, a former math professor, had definitely held back—or maybe exams so traumatized him, Jonny had not done well without trying, and his average was a modest safe 3.9.

Better to be a safe coward than a sorry hero. Why I'd thought such remarks were just stupid jokes kids made, I don't know.

Fact is, I had just not been thinking. Later in my life, or rather in my next life, as a university student, when I would be studying psychology, at least a primitive form of cognitive psychology, I would learn about the phenomenon of "attention"—"attentiveness"—that is within consciousness but is the pointed, purposeful, focused aspect of consciousness. Just to have your eyes open is to be conscious only minimally; to *pay attention* is something further. In my schoolgirl life I was conscious, but I was not *paying attention.* Focused on tasks like homework, exams, friends to sit with in cafeteria and hang out with in gym class, I did not pick up more than a fraction of what hovered in the air about me, the warnings of teachers that were non-verbal, glances that should have alerted me to—something.

I would realize, in my later life, that virtually all of my life beforehand had been *minimally conscious.* I had questioned virtually nothing, I had scarcely tried to decipher the precise nature of what my parents were actually trying to communicate to me, apart from their words. For my dear parents were *accursed with attentiveness.* I had taken them for granted—I had taken my own bubble-life for granted…

So it happened, Adriane Strohl was named valedictorian of her graduating class. Good news! Congratulations!

Now I assume that no one else who might've been qualified wanted this "honor"—just as no one else wanted a Patriot Democracy scholarship. Except there'd been some controversy, the school administration was said to favor another student for the honor of giving the valedictory address, not Adriane Strohl but a boy with a 4.2 average and also a varsity letter in football and a Good Democratic Citizenship Award, whose parents were allegedly of a higher caste than mine, and whose father was not MI but EE (a special distinction granted to Exiled persons who had served their terms of Exile and had been what was called 110 percent rehabilitated—Exile Elite).

I'd known about the controversy vaguely, as a school rumor. The EE father's son had not such high grades as I did, but it was believed that he would give a smoother and more entertaining valedictory address since his course of study was TV Public Relations and not the mainstream curriculum. And maybe administrators were concerned that Adriane Strohl would not be entertaining but would say "unacceptable" things in her speech?

Somehow without realizing, over a period of years, I'd acquired a reputation among my teachers and classmates for saying "surprising" things—"unexpected" things—that other students would not have said. Impulsively I'd raised my hands and asked questions. I was not *doubtful* exactly—just curious, and wanting to know. For instance was a "science fact" always and inevitably a fact? Did water *always* boil at 212 degrees F., or did it depend upon how pure the water was? And were boy-students *always* smarter than girl students, judging from actual tests and grades in our school?

Some of teachers (male) made jokes about me, so that the class laughed at my silly queries; other (female) teachers were annoyed, or maybe frightened. My voice was usually quiet and courteous but I might've come across as *willful.*

Sometimes the quizzical look in my face disconcerted my teachers, who took care always to compose their expressions when they stood in front of a classroom. There were approved ways of showing interest, surprise, (mild) disapproval, severity. (Our classrooms, like all public spaces and many private spaces, were "monitored for quality assurance" but adults were more keenly aware of surveillance than teenagers.)

Each class had its spies. We didn't know who they were, of course—it was said that if you thought you knew, you were surely mistaken since the DCVSB (Democratic Citizens Volunteer Surveillance Bureau) chose spies so carefully, it was analogous to the camouflage wings of a certain species of moth that blends in *seamlessly* with the bark of a certain tree. As Dad said *Your teachers can't help it. They can't deviate from the curriculum. The ideal is lock-step—each teacher in each classroom performing like a robot and never deviating from script under penalty of—you know what.*

(Was this true? For years in our class—the Class of NAS -23—there'd been vague talk of a teacher—how long ago, we didn't know—maybe when we were in middle school?—who'd "deviated" from the script one day, began talking wildly, and laughing, and shaking his/her fist at the "eye" (in fact, there were probably numerous "eyes" in any classroom, and all invisible), and was arrested, and overnight Deleted—so a new teacher was hired to take his/her place; and soon no one remembered the teacher-who'd-been-Deleted. And after a while we couldn't even remember clearly that one of our teachers *had been* Deleted. (Or had there been more than one? Were certain classrooms in our school *haunted?*) In our brains where the memory of XXXX [solid bar] should have been, there was just blank.

Definitely, I was not aggressive in class. I don't think so. But compared to my mostly meek classmates, some of whom sat small in their desks like partially folded-up papier-mache dolls, it is possible that Adriane Strohl stood out—in an unfortunate way.

In Patriot Democracy History, for instance, I'd questioned "facts" of history, sometimes. I'd asked questions about the subject no one ever questioned—the Great Terrorist Attacks of 9/11/01. But not in an arrogant way, really—just out of curiosity! I certainly didn't want to get any of my teachers in trouble with the EOB (Education Oversight Bureau) which could result in them being demoted or fired or—"vaporized."

I'd thought that, well—people liked me, mostly. I was the spiky-haired girl with the big glistening dark-brown eyes and a voice with a little catch in it and a habit of asking questions. Like a really young child with too much energy in kindergarten, you hope will run in circles and tire herself out. With a kind of naïve obliviousness I earned good grades so it was assumed that, despite my father being of MI caste, I would qualify for a federally-mandated State Democracy University.

(That is, I was eligible for admission to one of the massive state universities. At these, a thousand students might attend a lecture, and many courses were online.)

Restricted universities were far smaller, prestigious and inaccessible to all but a fraction of the population; though not listed online or in any public directory, these universities were housed on "traditional" campuses in Cambridge, New Haven, Princeton, etc., in restricted districts. Not only did we not know precisely where these centers of learning were, we had not ever met anyone with degrees from them.)

When in class I raised my hand to answer a teacher's question I often did notice classmates glancing at me—my friends, even—sort of uneasy, apprehensive—*What will Adriane say now? What is wrong with Adriane?*

There was nothing wrong with *me*! I was sure.

In fact, I was secretly proud of myself. Maybe just a little vain. Wanting to think *I am Eric Strohl's daughter.*

HOW STORIES MAKE THE WORLD

THE BAY AREA BOOK FESTIVAL
APRIL 29, 2018
BERKELEY, CALIFORNIA

ANTHONY MARRA (AM), ISMAIL MUHAMMAD (IM), JOYCE CAROL OATES (JCO), SCOTT SAUL (SS)

JOSEPH DI PRISCO (JDP), MODERATOR

JDP: Welcome, everybody. I'm Joe Di Prisco, Chair of the Simpson Family Literary Project. This is the panel where we'll be discussing how stories make the world. UC Berkeley Arts and Design is one sponsor. It's the campus-wide initiative led by Shannon Jackson, Associate Vice Chancellor for the Arts and Design. This is an initiative that seeks to feature and fortify our creative campus and to provide a ready vehicle for community partnership and public engagement, like with the Bay Area Festival of Books. The Simpson Family Literary Project [is the other sponsor, now] in its third year of operations. We support writing workshops taught at Contra Costa County Juvenile Hall, at Northgate High School, and at Girls Inc. in Downtown Oakland and the Writer in Residence program at the Lafayette Library and the $50,000 yearly award to a mid-career author of fiction.

So that's us. No applications [for the Simpson Prize] will be taken today, although we probably could get some pretty good applications if we did. All right, so let me introduce our distinguished panel. If I took the time to list every award and honor of everybody at this table, we would not get started til noon, so I'm not going to do that.

Over there, we have Scott Saul, an Americanist professor at UC Berkeley, author of a wonderful book, *Becoming Richard Pryor*. He'll be joining us to talk about everything. And then we have Ismail Muhammad, who's a Simpson fellow teaching at Contra Costa County Juvenile Hall. He's a terrific critic published in *The Paris Review* and elsewhere. I won't list all his publications, but well worth reading.

And then we have Anthony Marra, who was just named the second Simpson Prize winner, and has an armload of prizes to his credit. Author of *A Constellation of Vital Phenomena* and *The Tsar of Love and Techno*. And then this is someone you might recognize, Joyce Carol Oates. A giant in our world and I'm not even going to try to suggest what Joyce has done.

My plan as moderator is to ask a few questions and get out of the way of our speakers. I hope that they will engage each other in these questions and in the answers that they live as writers and teachers. Here we are, writers of different generations, races, and cultural backgrounds.

I'm pretty confident that the differences that we are sensitive to in our conversation will be instructive for everybody unless I totally mess this up, this conversation, which there is a good chance I'll do. All right, so the Simpson Literary Project has a mantra. You need one of those. Our mantra is "Storytelling is the foundation of a literate society."

So here you are, Joyce is on our project committee, Scott's on our project committee, Ismail who's a Simpson fellow, and Tony who just won the Simpson Prize. I would love to get your reactions, your responses to that mantra: "Storytelling is the foundation of a literate society." Who wants to go first, Scott?

SS: Okay. Well, I actually brought here a little quote from Walter Benjamin. It was a great essay called "Thee Storyteller" and it's about the threat to storytelling and how endangered it is. He wrote, "The art of storytelling is coming to an end. Less and less frequently do we encounter people with the ability to tell a tale properly." Here you might think about when you go to a café and you see a group of four people and each of them is on their phones not telling stories.

"More and more often there is embarrassment all around when the wish to hear a story is expressed. It is as if something that seemed inalienable to us, the securest among our possessions were taken from us: the ability to exchange experiences. One reason for this phenomenon is obvious: experience has fallen in value. And it looks as if it's continuing to fall into bottomlessness." Well, Walter Benjamin wrote that in the aftermath of World War I. And so the question is, was that true then? Now does this still pertain?

I personally think that we live in a world that's full of information, that was Walter Benjamin's analysis as well, where information streams into us and we live in this media unlimited society. I think that there's a difference between information, processing information which we become very good at like human computers, and the ability to craft a story and to inhabit experience and to try to reach out to other people's experience. So I'll start there.

JCO: Just to expand on that, it's an interesting quote, but if it had been uttered at the end of World War I, it's the very cusp of the great modernist 20th century. I mean, look at the brilliant work that's coming in poetry, art, music, everything. I'm just not sure how relevant… Though the quote in itself is provocative and interesting, historically it seems to have been mistaken and also the storytelling, say of Nazi Germany, that's a kind of malicious storytelling. We would say totally fiction. The Aryan cosmology is totally fictitious, but it is a storytelling that many people believed in. So just to respond to that.

JDP: Yeah, but again, literacy and literature, people make a distinction here. I wonder if, Ismail, you're teaching at Contra Costa County Juvie. Do you feel that literature and literacy are a unified goal?

IM: Can you repeat the question for me?

JDP: No. I can't, actually, but I'll make up another one. People make a distinction, well, if you want to promote literacy, it's not about storytelling. Storytelling is an advanced form of literacy. One of the underlying assumptions of the Project is, well, one way that kids become literate is by telling their stories. I mean, Joyce has a wonderful story about becoming a writer before she knew how to write. Before she knew words, she was writing stories. I don't even know what that means, but I believe it.

JCO: I was scribbling.

JDP: Scribbling. Okay. Chickens and stuff. Okay. So, Ismail.

IM: Yeah. I just had my first session at this juvenile detention facility last Tuesday.

IM: What struck me was that I don't know what these kids' lives are like at all. I have not had their experiences at all, so I'm letting them guide me through what they want the class to be, the workshop to be at this point. One of the first things they did was ask me to show a music video, a Bay Area rap artist named Mazi, who I had never heard of.

I had never heard of this song before, but I was open to watching the video and letting them explain to me what about the song seemed to reflect their world. One of the students after we watched it ended up making a connection between that video and a poem we had read that day. It's Danez Smith's "Alternate Names for Black Boys." It's a gorgeous poem written in the wake of Black Lives Matter.

It just struck me that literature and literacy are working toward a unified goal. We should be careful about what we think about as being literature and what forms of media or storytelling help encourage literacy in youth and in what ways they actually see their stories being told in the public. I wonder if we can broaden our ideas of what literature can be. I can't help but remark that Kendrick Lamar just won the Pulitzer Prize for music. Was it a few weeks ago?

SS: Ismail has a great piece about that, in *Slate*. Check it out.

IM: It's in *Slate*. It came out last week. Read it.

AM: Yeah. I think it's, for me, there was a priest who told me when I was a kid that compassion is the ability to see someone else's suffering in you and to see your suffering in someone else. I think that storytelling is the means of transmitting that information. I think for me the goal of literature or one of its aims besides the pure aesthetic experience is this question of making a more just and humane space for people to encounter one another. That, to me, is sort of the endpoint of literature, to create these places where books serve almost as tunnels that can drop you through the center of the earth and you can emerge besides people you would never otherwise meet and recognize yourself in them.

JDP: Following up here, not to go all writer conferencey, Squaw Valley or Bread Loaf or something, but Joy Williams said something the other day that I found interesting. She said, "The work of a writer is to keep the story from becoming what it is about." It made me think of Vivian Gornick's terrific book, *The Situation and the Story*. I don't know if you guys are familiar with that brilliant book, but I'm wondering. Does that kind of reading resonate for you as teachers or as writers? That is, your job as a writer is to keep the story from being what it is about and to be the story?

SS: I'll speak as a biographer.

You notice there's a lot of biographies that are extremely long. Sometimes they seem to suffer from an excess of information that hasn't been digested into a story and that's a problem. I think that a lot of great biographies, you see that they have a little preface that's like five to ten pages where they basically say, "Oh, this is kind of what it's about." They establish that, but then after that, you just get immersed in the story.

Anyway, the argument that the biographer is making about the person's life is threaded through the story. I think those are the biographies that live, that where you feel like this, you're seeing the character of the person whose biography you're reading come alive. You see it from different angles. You see who they might have become, who they didn't become, how their relationships shaped them. I think that's what gives those biographies that kind of beating heart that as opposed to just being a mass of information.

JDP: And that's what footnotes are for.

SS: There you go. Love the footnotes. You got to love the footnotes.

JDP: You have a hundred pages of footnotes in *Becoming Richard Pryor*.

AM: This question about what a story is about, I think that is often something that the reader of a book almost brings to it more than the writer, and I'd be fascinated to hear your experiences with it, Joyce. I often feel that the book's controlling themes and the sort of philosophical or political or those sort of cultural textures that a book ultimately becomes about only emerges well into the process of writing or even in the final stages. That if you go into a project thinking I'm going to make an argument about this in the manner that you would with an essay, the novel feels essayistic and perhaps slightly inert and losing that kind of wonderful realness that a good piece of fiction I think provides.

JCO: Yes. Well, we can think of literature as along a spectrum. At one extreme, you have works that seem very objective and they're maybe filled with history and with research and the world is very vividly presented. This may be very commercially successful fiction. They're novels that take us to places, like travelogues. If you read them carefully and immerse yourself in them, it's really almost as if you are there.

So there's a high degree of what it's about, a high degree of information. As we move along the spectrum, you come into different kinds of voices and different sorts of perspectives, especially in the 20th century which is a very experimental century. Right now we have storytelling that would almost be incomprehensible to our ancestors.

We have wonderfully radical, idiosyncratic first-person monologues that may be published in *The New Yorker*, for instance. Stories like that are utterances that are very unique and sometimes very funny. Some of them are like standup comedy because that's another genre of our era, like rap music. These are all expressions of human creativity. As we move along in that direction, the degree of information or what it's about gets smaller and smaller.

It's more and more about a person, about a voice, about maybe a really wonderful voice or it could be an obnoxious, annoying voice but still you love to hate that voice. The idea of the writer as performer or presenter in contrast with, as I said at the beginning, the different kind of novel that's very believable and honest, a sort of honest novel companion of history and facts and contrast with more experimental work that's sort of moving through the middle.

Novels like the great novels of William Faulkner, which are not immediately accessible to many readers and back in the 18th or 19th century would have been maybe incoherent and unintelligible. Now we can read those novels, especially if we've gone to UC Berkeley and studied in the English Department, but you do need a kind of training to get into this more experimental work. That's what Joy Williams meant. Joy Williams herself is a very experimental and sort of weirdly wonderful writer who many people could read and say, "Well, what was that about?"

JDP: I want to quote something that T. Geronimo Johnson wrote. Geronimo was the 2017 Simpson Prize winner. He wrote, "In more recent years, American writers have written boldly across divides of class, age, ethnic identity, and gender. We must trust the human imagination, its predilection for digging at the roots of things, for prying at what is fixed. We must hesitate to suggest boundaries and perimeters. Let us strive to dissolve borders." So my question for my distinguished panel is, specifically when it comes to race and ethnicity, topics you've all addressed in various ways, does Geronimo's takeaway mean something to you about borders?

IM: I'm hesitant to valorize the idea of dissolving borders. I sympathize with the notion that we want to collapse the distance between various racial or ethnic or religious or gender identities and kind of as Anthony said, drop ourselves beside people who we don't understand initially, but I wonder if there's a better metaphor for that experience than dissolving borders between us. Does that mean ... or implicit in that metaphor, at least to me, is the idea of dissolving identity. Something about that just doesn't appeal to me.

I think of DuBois in *Souls of Black Folks*. He talks about unity in alterity, which is a great metaphor for me for what it means to be American, to think about literature in the American context. The idea that you can be a single people or think about one another's experiences while maintaining space for that difference or that alterity. I don't think that necessitates dissolving borders between us, necessarily. The borders are what help us recognize and think about each other's differences and therefore hopefully become more empathetic and more understanding.

JDP: What are the challenges representing race/ethnicity these days, then? What are the metaphors that the rest of you would use?

SS: I just speak as a biographer trying to write the story of Richard Pryor. He grew up in a brothel in Peoria, Illinois. I grew up in the suburbia of San Fernando Valley in the seventies. Very different and…some people would say. Although actually interestingly enough, his daughter lived a block down from me when I was zero to ten years old. I had no idea. Anyway, and actually there was a lot of craziness going on just a block away from me in that world, but I didn't see it.

I was thinking there is other people who wrote about Pryor who would just, in the middle of the biography, they would just be in his head. They'd be in the experience as a way to animate the biography and give it a real sense of life. I was like, "Wait, there's no footnotes here. How do they actually know this?" I felt like unless I had…for a biographer, this is very different from the practice of a fiction writer, I think.

I didn't want to presume to be able to get into his head. I wanted to interview people who knew him to reconstruct their sense of certain encounters or if I had his own writing. I tried to be judicious about that boundary. On the other hand, I wouldn't have invested eight years of my life if I didn't actually really want to understand his own experience and try to recapture it for people.

I think to answer the question about the dissolving of borders, I feel like we should throw ourselves into trying to understand other people's experience. We should also be willing to do the work that is required. It's not like you can just sit in your easy chair and suddenly you're there. That's part of it, but there also, I think there is you can't just by fiat, be there. I don't want to denigrate the power of the imagination, which is so awesome, especially amongst the people who are on this panel. But I do think it's a challenge rather than just an open invitation.

JDP: Well, this goes to a point that you were making, Ismail, about how perhaps storytelling or teaching storytelling is all about introducing the defamiliarization of the world. It assists students to have their world defamiliarized before their very eyes by, through storytelling. Did I get what you said?

IM: Um…

JDP: No, probably not.

IM: No, I mean, I—

JDP: Would anybody else like to do this panel here?

IM: You're doing a great job. No, I do think that that to me as somebody who's currently teaching a creative writing workshop and as a writer, that's the chief value of storytelling is that it makes our world unfamiliar to us. It takes received narratives or preconceived notions and distorts them somewhat into shapes that we might vaguely recognize and forces us to rethink how we move through the world, how we think about other people, how we pursue knowledge.

Yeah, that's what I'm trying to convey to my students in the juvenile detention facility now. These are kids who, or youth, rather, who have had many narratives attached to them and their bodies and probably perceive their lives as being somewhat constricted and predetermined. I want them to be able to read and write to break out of those constrictions.

JDP: Following up on that, Scott has written a terrific book about Richard Pryor, getting into his head to whatever extent that's true. Ismail's written very memorably about James Baldwin, about Cornel West and his battle with Ta-Nehisi Coates. Tony has dealt with Chechnyans and as he said recently, no publisher in New York was looking for the next great novel relating to Chechnya, so he provided two.

So you've dealt with issues of ethnicity and of a very radical sort. Joyce, you've dealt with these issues of alterity dramatically. I mean even in the most recent, the *LA Times* prize-winning book, *The Book of American Martyrs* where you open up the world of both sides or the multiple sides of the abortion debate. What do we do with that? You started this. You guys wrote the books. I'm just talking about them.

SS: Can I follow up on your question, Joe, for Joyce and Tony? I'm always questioned like, how do writers choose the point of view that they'll use? With you, you both do remarkable things shifting point of view. Joyce, I think about your story about Robert Frost, in *Harper's*. It generated a little controversy, but that's good, where it begins through the first person perspective of a woman visiting Robert Frost. By the last part, we're in the third person.

Tony, you do a lot of thing with different points of view. Right now I'm reading a great new novel by Julian Barnes. You should all read it. It's called *The Only Story* and the first section is written from the first person point of view. There's section two written from the second person point of view, section three written from the third person point of view. Check it out.

JCO: It's a deal.

SS: When does one decide that you need a different kind of focalization? Is that part of the plan when you start or is it, it emerges as you're organically writing a story? You realize, "I need to just shift things around"? How do you come to those decisions?

JCO: Well, I think that it depends upon what sort of novel you're undertaking. If it's somewhat experimental, then I think you're free to move around easily and without apology to Henry James or anyone like that to move from different perspectives following the arc of the story. It's like a light illumination here, the story's moving along and you want to be there. If it's maybe a more conventional or traditional work of fiction, you would probably stay with one point of view.

Julian Barnes is an experimental writer. He's a great modernist writer. That's very playful and Nabokovian. That's what he's doing and that really appeals to me because I'm a formalist essentially.

AM: For me at least, I usually spend most of the writing process trying to figure out what that point of view is. With my first novel, *A Constellation of Vital Phenomena*, it took me four drafts to sort of stumble into this omniscient perspective. It makes me think of the quote that you started off with. It seems like around that same time, shortly after World War II, we sort of abandoned omniscience as a viable and honest form of narration. That God is dead and we shouldn't trust any authority that has that seemingly false sense of knowledge and omnipotence.

I think over the last maybe ten, twenty, twenty-five years omniscience maybe has come to the fore once again and it's a form of narration that I personally am drawn to and have used in both of my books. It seems that in the same way that omniscience may have captured the perspective of societies in which God was omniscient.

We now live in a world where we are all omniscient. We all have little machines in our pockets that can find any amount of information from any source at any time in any place. There's something about this seemingly antiquated mode of storytelling that actually feels incredibly prescient and feels very well suited to our current era.

JCO: But the twenty-first century use of omniscience is very different from the traditional because you have this playful point of view. Cormac McCarthy, for instance has a very ironic, almost biblical omniscient point of view. Maybe a little Nabokovian, where there's a little spin of irony that tempers the tenderness and the horror and sympathy we might feel for our characters is sort of tempered by a little bit of dissonance and a little bit of distance. But Dickens had that same sort of freewheeling slightly comic ironic omniscient point of view. I think that it's very bold and original.

I usually warn students not to try to do that because as you said, it took you four drafts. You have to have a tone that's Olympian but not sarcastic or superior seeming. You have to be able to suggest some sympathy but not sentimentality. Whereas if you're writing from the first person point of view, you don't have to think about any of those things. You basically have your voice.

Great novels of all kinds that we've written from the first person point of view. Thinking of *Huckleberry Finn,* for instance. Maybe that's our greatest novel from that point of view.

I'm sorry. I'm sort of blanking out on some other examples... Harper Lee, *To Kill a Mockingbird*, that's another good example. I was thinking of young adult novels that pass for adult novels and those twowould be in that category.

JDP: So what about the new voices and the new cultures that are entering into the literary conversation? How have they changed the way we tell and listen to stories? Are you encouraged by prevailing trends in publishing, reviewing, and writing? Any examples come to mind about books that are novels, stories that are written these days that could have never been written thirty years ago, and lead the way to a new kind of dialogue in the literary world, and beyond?

IM: I think probably the best and most entertaining book and the most affecting book I've read in the last five years has been Yaa Gyasi, *Homegoing*. I'm sure many of you have read it. Just because it accomplishes something that I've never seen done in contemporary African American Literature, which is to try to create this massive fictional artifice of a Black Diasporic History that begins in one place and ends in America, which is not something that most African Americans can claim. Nobody really knows who their ancestors are in West Africa. So, it's definitely a work of fantasy. There's something fantastical about it, something fantastical even in the idea of wanting to figure out what your origins are on the other side of the Atlantic, but I think it's a great work of a fiction and kind of interesting intervention into how we think about Black history. I can't imagine that being done thirty years ago.

AM: I've been really taken recently with novels that try to address technological changes. We were talking yesterday…I've been talking to everyone. I've been a broken record on it, but there's a new book by Richard Powers called *The Overstory*, which is one of the most profound books I've read in a very long time. It's a novel about trees. He addresses, in interviews and within the book, he talks about how traditionally American literature has been focused on psychological conflicts and that every now and then books will step into the conflicts with society. But that very rarely do books venture into environmental conflicts, the largest kind of conflict that a human can be part of. This is an incredible gap in our literature that we're not addressing even as the evidence of climate change is abundant and rampant, that fiction doesn't address or rarely addresses, seems unsuited to address these large-scale environmental conflicts because it moves at a pace that few individual people can really comprehend and hold in their head the way we can much more intimate conflicts between characters.

I feel like that book, *The Overstory*, is just revolutionary in terms of making environmental conflict the center of the book above all of the messy drama of human hearts. To pull it off in a way that makes you care about trees even more than the characters who are obsessed with them, I think is a real triumph.

JCO: There's a novel I have not read in a while by Barbara Gowdy called I think *The White Bone*. That's about a family of elephants. When I mention it to people their eyes sort of glaze over like they don't really want to read a novel about a family of elephants.

I found it such a profound and deeply moving novel. I'm sitting here yearning to reread it. I have to wait until I get back home to Princeton to read it. Maybe that's a little bit like this though the family of elephants is concerned with how to survive and of course terrible things happen to some of the elephants you get to care about. So in a way it replicates some of the human drama.

This novel by Richard Powers I understand is about overarching trees, like over a house, a family house?

AM: The book itself… And this sounds ridiculous, but it's structured like a tree. It begins with this section called "Roots" that has the various back stories of these characters. Then the trunk where their stories all collide and then the crest, where they culminate in the seed telling the aftermath of their lives.

JCO: How long is it?

AM: It's about five hundred pages, I think.

It's long, but the main characters are really trees in a way that seems impossible to do. I think decades ago, even a few years ago, you wouldn't… The science simply wasn't there in enough abundance to really pull it off.

SS: Just to respond to Joe's original question about storytelling and what are the seeds that are [cultivated today]… I think about *Hamilton*. That song, who lives, who dies, who tells your story as spoken by Eliza. We don't have the fragments of our past. I think that's a question [for] a lot of young people who love

Hamilton especially a lot of young women, young girls who love it. They're taking this question on for themselves. There's such an efflorescence of young adult literature out there that I think is much more experimental and wide-ranging than it's been in the past. So many young readers who are thinking, "Who is gonna tell my story?" I think this is a wonderful sign. I think the national story is getting rewritten through *Hamilton* or wonderful play that is coming back to Cal Shakes. People should go see it called *Black Odyssey*.

JDP: It's a great play.

SS: Which retells the story of *The Odyssey* from the point of the view of a Black veteran of the Afghanistan War. Incredible. I think that we are in a wonderful moment of storytelling as well as a horrible moment of national politics. We need these stories to help bring people together.

JDP: I'm very involved with Cal Shakes, and it's also the funniest scene ever played by a car, a great car scene.

You brought up *Hamilton*. We've been talking about literary storytelling, but what are your thoughts about other kinds of storytelling? The movies, TV, how is this kind of storytelling connecting differently, or similarly to our literary fictions? Really want to know, what are your favorite TV shows.

JCO: I just want to amplify Joe's excellent question by saying about two weeks ago, Angela Davis gave a presentation on campus and she said something that was so powerful and it really sort of brought tears to my eyes. She said, I think she was being interviewed onstage, she was asked about social justice and how activists should act and so forth. She said, "Sometimes I think that the artist does the most important work in advancing the cause of social justice by making us feel before we know what we have said." By making us feel something that maybe we will say, I thought that was so beautiful. That applies to all these different genres whether it's television, film, music, literature.

JDP: What's your favorite TV show, Joyce?

JCO: I'm not sure I have a favorite. My husband and I watch series, like we're watching *The Americans*, which I thought was very powerfully done and shaping into being a tragedy as it unfolds.

I think it's a tragedy of misplaced idealism and in the beginning we sort of went along with it. A little like *Breaking Bad,* where the protagonist starts off somewhat sympathetically, quite sympathetically and then he evolves becomes more and more like a monster. So slowly that she doesn't seem to understand and maybe some viewers don't quite understand how that could happen. You turn into a monster.

JDP: Anthony, I know you spend some time in LA. Give it up.

AM: What I was thinking when you asked the question was if you read anything by Dostoevsky you can tell that he's never seen a TV show before. Imagine trying to adapt a chapter of Dostoevsky. Back to one of your earlier comments of how books that are writing today that couldn't have been written earlier. I think probably a lot of the narrative styles that we've become accustomed to now in novels owe a good deal to movies. The fact that the present tense has become a pretty popular tense to narrate in compared to a hundred years ago. Seems to be in no small part drawn from the way that we experience film. The fact that we talk about scenes within chapters. The fact that so much pressure now is put on… There's a readerly expectation to have novels that are largely composed of scenes in a way that say Dostoevsky, his work has less scenes and more sort of ten-page monologues.

But in terms of works that I've been particularly drawn to. Generally speaking TV is a much more exciting place now than the movie theater. It used to be that a movie… That the novel was sort of almost this über art form where you could do more in a novel than you could in a ninety-minute or two-hour film. But now with these television shows that run for six or seven seasons, it dwarfs what a novel is capable of purely in terms of narrative reach.

I recently watched *Babylon Berlin*, which is this crazy take on Weimar-Germany. It would've taken a 3,000-page book to fit what they managed to do over the course of a couple of seasons in there.

Just the scope of some of those projects even when they go a bit haywire, I think is pretty magnificent.

JDP: So you're not watching *This is Us* or *Rosanne*?

AM: I don't have a TV. I only have a computer. So, it has to go to Netflix first.

JDP: All right, come on, favorite TV shows.

IM: I've always been struck by the reasons why I watch TV. I watch television and film for very different reasons than I read a book. I want literature to pull my world apart and question my identity and the way the world is structured. I watch TV shows because I want to see my experience reflected on the screen. In that sense, a TV show like *Insecure*. I love it. I'm from Los Angeles. I'm from South Central so I watch *Insecure* and I'm like "Those are Black people and that's my hometown." That makes me feel good. I don't often feel that with literature.

When I do get that with literature, I feel suspicious immediately. If I read a book that "perfectly reflects" my experience, I'm going to throw it across the room immediately. I just-

JDP: How'd they find that stuff out…

IM: Exactly, right.

But that being said, the TV show I'm most excited about right now is *Atlanta* by Donald Glover-

JDP: Yes, that's a great show—

IM: Incredible achievement.

JDP: "Robbin' Season."

IM: Yeah, "Robbin' Season."

IM: As if Richard Wright had been transposed to Atlanta in 2018, it's alternately tragic and hilarious. Even the title, "Robbin'

Season," I like the fact that it can either be about a singing robin or about the season in Atlanta where people being robbing each other because as Christmas approaches they need money to buy presents for their families.

He's working at that level of literary depth that you don't see on television that often. He's also a rapper, intriguingly. If you haven't been watching *Atlanta*, you should. It's great.

JDP: Scott, you're a pop culture guy.

SS: In terms of seeing your experience reflected back at you, maybe for me it's through a convex mirror. It's *Transparent*, which I feel really captured the texture of Jewish family life in LA. I was totally drawn into it.

I just taught a class on the seventies and we saw *Network*. Where Howard Beale gives a monologue, the one after the most famous one, where's he's about "Turn it off, turn it off, turn off those TVs, you're becoming humanoids."

Although I feel there's almost a super-abundance of seductive programming now on TV, and it's easy to change one's habits so that at eleven o'clock instead of picking up a novel, and reading that, you can just put on a show that has three seasons and you're gonna probably stay awake longer watching the TV show and binge.

Actually I'm trying to not be seduced by that super-abundance because I do feel like there's a gratification I get from being in the pages of a novel or a biography, what have you, that to me is more deeply fulfilling. I've started to somehow question how TV fulfills my appetites.

I love noir. There's so much amazing Italian noir, Scandinavia noir... All these great detective shows but at a certain point you realize, "Why am I watching another show about a serial killer who does some horrible things to women's bodies."

At some point you just flip it off and you decide "I'm gonna tell myself a different story." I think this is something that Joyce brought up at the very beginning of the panel. There are many different kinds of stories we can tell ourselves. Sometimes you need to switch the story, like switching the channel. That I think can be a very deliberate move you make to change your life.

JDP: But let's go back to the public role of the author. How has that changed in your minds these days? With the Amazon Industrial Complex? With print on demand? With self-publishing? How has the public role of the author changed? Maybe the corollary question, how has the role of the audience changed with the arrival of these new forms of delivery of stories?

JCO: I think there is a very public voice and then there's always a small, private voice. The great poets of the 19th Century were Walt Whitman and Emily Dickinson, and one was extremely public and he saw himself as a sort of exemplar and he represented all of human kind basically. Talking about himself as a way of talking about all of us, but he talked about many, many things. Walt Whitman was a great poet of egalitarianism and love between people, not necessarily opposite sex, but just a great love, brotherhood, sisterhood. Love of animals, love of life. He was solidly immersed in history. He has very beautiful short lyrics also, but we think of him and these long lines, incantatory, and hypnotic.

But then Emily Dickinson was very private. I'm not saying that one is masculine and one is feminine. It sort of seems that way. But neither one of them is to be defined by his or her gender because Whitman had a good deal about the female in him. And Emily Dickinson is very sharp and cerebral, has a good deal of what we might call "the masculine."

But as it turned out, Emily Dickinson was a very private person. She wrote small poems, small in outline, but very dynamic and universal and deep in content. It seems to me that there's a role for the public personality if that is your extroverted self and you want to get into "the scrimmage of life," as D. H. Lawrence said.

But if you're not like that, I don't see any reason why you should force yourself and nobody should criticize you. You want to be very private, have your own poetry, your own private thoughts, you don't want to engage with the politics of the time, I think that's perfectly respectable and I don't think anyone should tell anyone else what to do.

So there's a role for the quiet, beautiful work of art that just maybe speaks to a very few people or as time goes one, like Emily Dickinson's poetry, which was not published as you know during her time, eventually that maybe even outshines the more public work.

SS: I can speak, thinking as a teacher, something that I've observed and that's been actually documented by this very interesting study. I think it's called the "Stanford Writing Study." They looked at Stanford students and how they thought about their own writing. And, I've noticed this change as well. My fifteen-plus years as a teacher, is that, used to be you would give students an assignment, and they were writing it for you. You read it, you graded it, it's done.

And that seemed more and more dead as a way of understanding writing. Students these days, they want to write for a certain audience. Writing that is only gonna be filed away for a grade seems much less vital to them. I think of the Stanford study, this idea that you style yourself differently while writing for different audiences. And, that the younger generation, I think is very good at this. They understand when you're texting one person you have a different voice than when you're composing an email to this other person.

I think that people who are not certainly authors, yet. But I think people already have a sense more that writing exists to do something in the world, to activate possibilities in the world. That I think is generally a very good thing.

JDP: Our poetry students tend to read poems online. They don't tend to buy books. They have a different connection to the text. Is that a good thing? Is that a complicated thing? Is it inevitable and we'll all live with it, and it works to our advantage ultimately?

AM: I think it's a bad thing if you want poets to continue to exist, and to be able—

JDP: So that's a no.

AM: —to put food on the table and a roof over their head. I think that of all the wondrous things that technology gives us, the depreciation and value of cultural creation, I think, is a real hazard, that when you can consume everything for free, what you consume no longer has any value. I think that's incredibly frightening thinking down the line, in terms of it's not a sustainable model of artistic practice.

IM: I have another perception of that. I think as somebody who is still in the early stages of my career and still hustling, I feel that devaluation really strongly, and that people aren't willing to pay for writing, as they were in the past. Also, I think as somebody who is active on Twitter, or uses Instagram, uses Facebook, and Tumblr, or stuff like that, there is great pleasure in being a reader or a viewer in this age, in that Twitter and the internet have allowed ways of engaging with culture and art that simply weren't possible before.

Roland Barthes, he makes the distinction between the writerly text and the readerly text, with the writerly text being that which allows the writer to impose an idea or an experience on his or their audience, and of readerly text, being that which allows their reader to wander through the text and construct their own… To put together a narrative via actual effort, as opposed to being given a narrative.

I feel like that's what Twitter does. You're being handed poems, maybe unmoored from a single text, and the poet is not being paid for your experience of reading that poem, but there's something about reading that poem while you have another tab open to a music video, and another tab open to maybe *Atlanta*, and then another tab open to some kind of Tumblr feed that you find really intriguing, that creates an aesthetic experience that simply wasn't possible before the Internet, and redounds to different ways of creating art as well.

It hurts us, but also, I think it vastly expands what's possible, in terms of creating art and experiencing art, just to protect Silicon Valley. They need protection.

JDP: It needs a lot of "protection." Not to go all Oprah here... Well, because Oprah's got her hands full about to run the country, and somehow some coalition of Oprah, Parkland High School students, and Stormy Daniels, maybe we can save the country.

We've been talking about being a writer, or writing, or doing the work of writing. I'm wondering, maybe you've had conversations the way I've had with students who say they want to be writers. Now, I've never met anybody who's ever taken any advice about love or writing, but maybe you have. I wonder, what is your response to some younger person, or older person, for that matter, who comes to you and says, "I really want to write. This is my vocation." How do you respond to that?

JCO: I think it's very rare that someone comes with such a raw appeal. It may usually be a young person who is already writing, who has been taking courses, so there is just sort of a gradual feeling, but I would never presume to predict the future for anyone. Writing is a difficult life. It may be very pleasurable to write, but to have a career, I think, is fraught with much anxiety.

We have Anthony Marra on this panel, who represents, I must say, .0001% of the young writers of his generation, because it isn't at all easy to have a life, to make a life, to continue.

My friend, Paul Auster, said he glanced around the other day, and he saw that virtually everyone who had started off with him, maybe in college or graduate school, who were writing and even beginning to publish are virtually all gone. Just a few of us, he said, are sort of trudging along that road now. He said, "Joyce, you're one of them."

It was a chilling thing, because I do remember all the very talented, and idealistic, and hopeful young people when I was young, who just maybe published a little bit, or a book or two, and then they fade out. It's not that they've failed exactly, but it's a hard life.

IM: I've been getting that question a lot in the last month, because I'm doing this mentorship, fellowship at Cal right now. A lot of my students, they're English majors and they want to be writers in the future. They're just like, "How do I actually make that happen at all, considering people don't pay, and there are very few platforms for writing?" My advice is always, "Go to grad school. Get your MFA or go to a PhD program, and just write when you have the security, and shelter, and time, and intellectual company that grad school supplies." It's not a perfect solution, but that kind of institution or patronage, it's been crucial for me.

SS: It's funny to me to hear you say that, because my students sometimes come to me, and they want to go to grad school, and I say, "Don't go to grad school." Maybe that's the one little escape clause, the loophole, is if you just want to be a writer, you're not thinking that actually I'm gonna get a job teaching with a PhD, because unfortunately, we're not supporting public higher education as we once did. I think that would make sense.

I think that is actually the best way to go to grad school, is to think, "Okay, the fellowship package is the most elaborate first book contract I could ever get, with all these crazy stipulations about all these other things I need to write along with that first book," and then meanwhile, you're gonna do some other writing along it, and be living, basically, on the edge of poverty the whole time.

JDP: Then you're remaindered as a graduate student at some point.

JCO: Can I ask a question? Of a biographer, I would think that of all those genres, biography is really fraught with a lot of pitfalls, because it means investing your time in years of research, and then hoping at the end, it could be five, six, seven, eight years, and then hoping that it will, first of all, be published, and then do well.

SS: This is why I have not... If you'll ask me what's my next book, I'm like, "Well..." There's so many pitfalls along the way. You have to deal with the states. The first event I did for my Richard Pryor book was a panel at the CUNY Center for Biography with Gary Giddins, who's written some beautiful books on Bing Crosby and jazz figures.

The other person on the panel was Mark Whitaker, who had just published a biography of Bill Cosby. He spent many years of his life writing this, and one of the things is that I felt for Mark Whitaker because he talked about he was from a biracial family. He didn't really know his black father, didn't have much of a relationship with him, if I'm getting this story right.

He was living, I think, in upstate Massachusets with this white mother, growing up in the eighties, and Bill Cosby was kind of a surrogate father figure through *The Cosby Show*. Then he became a very wonderful journalist, and did all these things, and he was gonna write the biography of Bill Cosby. Because Bill Cosby was living, there were certain conditions if he wanted to enter into the Cosby citadel and get access to friends, to hear basic stories about Bill Cosby's life.

He wrote a biography that had some strings attached. I think this was the last public event he did about the Bill Cosby biography, because the Hannibal Buress [rape comments about Cosby] circulated around that time, and the book now just cannot stand. It's all to say, it's often better to choose people who have died. It allows people to talk much more freely about that person, and that person can't sue you. This is really important.

Anyway, it is difficult. I think that I feel for any biographer who invests so much time in the life of somebody else to try to lovingly recreate or eventually, oftentimes full of so many mixed, ambivalent emotions, try to recreate that life.

JCO: There were a number of biographers who tried to write about Sylvia Plath. I know one or two of them, and it's a great subject, but just fraught with so much difficulty because of the estate. She's dead, but the estate lives on.

JDP: Well, I think we have some time for a few questions or comments.

S1: [Speaker 1] If you have a question, please come up to this blue line right here on the floor.

A1: [Audience Member 1] Now I know I've got the vapors.

Yes, I would love you to comment on audio books. Audible books, audio books, I'm finding that as my eyes age, I really like the audible template. Also, I'm relating to the story differently than if I were to read it. Now I want to go back and reread Joyce Carol Oates' books from about twenty, thirty years ago, because if they were read to me, they'd be much more graphic, and perverse. I first read them as a twenty-something-year-old, but perhaps you could fill us in about what direction this is taking literature, and is this a new frontier?

JDP: Of course, books have always had a performative dimension. Charles Dickens, he was the Mick Jagger of his day. What about the audio performance or types of performance when it comes to your work?

AM: I love audio books. I always have a couple going on. This is maybe after the reading or the binge-watching at night. I always go to sleep listening to an audio book. It's this very soothing, I feel like I'm a kid again, being read a bedtime story. There's something that they're almost all people with English accents who sound nothing like my Minnesotan mom, but there's something about the experience that really draws me back to that sense of just being lulled by storytelling that I find missing in other forms of my engagement with literature.

I think it also offers up this opportunity for almost like an old radio drama, where the performance aspect really comes to the fore. I haven't, but I would think that listening to Shakespeare or to plays might be a sort of more expansive experience than simply reading it on the page. I think they're terrific.

SS: I actually used audio books in my teaching of literature, because I find that it allows students often to engage with a story in ways that's harder otherwise. One incredible audiobook that you really must all download is *The Invisible Man* by Ralph Ellison, performed by Joe Morton, the actor.

It is just amazing. There's these scenes in *Invisible Man* that have ten different characters, and he's bringing them all to life. A scene that's almost chaotic on the page becomes just like what you're saying, just vivid drama.

I think also of another incredible audiobook is by Prodigy, the late rapper from Mobb Deep. I think there are ways that in certain audiobooks, especially some memoir recited by the author, you really get a sense of the grain of the voice. It adds a whole other dimension to the experience. I really think it's so wonderful that we have so many great performers of audiobooks.

JDP: Not to mention, we need to be more sensitive to learning differences and bypass strategies when it comes to students with executive function challenges.

SS: Or dyslexia.

S2: [Speaker 2] I'm wondering, in our information age, there seems to be tons of stories that we can orient ourselves around, or there's tons of religions and we just have a lot of stories that we can attach to ourselves. It seems that a lot of these stories…there are so many of them that it can be almost arbitrary which ones we live by.

I'm wondering, how can we find a story for ourselves? There's just so many, it seems, out there that different ideologies, so how can we find one that's right or …

JDP: You're looking for some guidance about where to look, inside yourself and outside yourself, for those stories that will give you meaning, give you direction?

S2: [Speaker 2] Yeah.

JDP: Several answers occur to me, but read a lot. That would be one thing, which I'm sure you do. I would say read where you find yourself most challenged, and where you've had a little difficulty getting through. Some of the most interesting reading experiences for me have been with writers whom I couldn't read the first time, or the first 10 times through.

JCO: I'll quote Toni Morrison. She said, "If you can't find the book that you want to read, you must write it yourself."

JDP: That's true.

SS: I actually brought a quote from Rebecca Solnit, who's speaking later. Everybody should go see her. In her amazing book, *The Faraway Nearby*, she writes, "We think we tell stories, but stories often tell us, tell us to love or to hate, to see or to be blind. Often, too often, stories saddle us, ride us, whip us onward, tell us what to do, and we do it without questioning. The task of learning to be free requires learning to hear them, to question them, to pause and hear silence, to name them, and then to become the storyteller."

JDP: Thank you for your question. I hope that was helpful. Is there another question?

S3: [Speaker 3] I read an article a couple of months ago, I think, by [inaudible] in *The New York Times*. He was saying that one of the basic rules about writing is show, don't tell. In this article, he said if you come from a culture that it's basically telling and not showing. That stayed with me, because I'm from Brazil, and I come from a culture that people tell and don't show that much.

I'm writing here, and all the rules about writing help me a lot, but my culture is different, and I just would like you to tell what you think about that.

JDP: Show versus tell, rules for writing. How do we approach rules for writing? I'm asking for a friend.

SS: I'll just say that there's a great book by Phillip Lopate called *To Show and To Tell*. I use it for teaching nonfiction. It's specifically about creative non-fiction, and how we should not denigrate the telling part, as well as the showing, that they work very well in sync, or in conjunction with one another.

JCO: Yes, I think just balance the pace of the narrative. Some writers have a lot of expository material and they tell a good deal, but they tell it so beautifully that we want to read it... Thomas Hardy, for instance, or Dickens, Faulkner. Hemingway doesn't have that. There's almost no expository material, and Hemingway just moves smoothly along in the present tense.

It's basically the sort of writing that is dramatizing and showing Hemingway's way of presenting the material. He's showing you what it is, what the scene is, but he's not telling what to think about it.

There's another kind of narration that frankly, does kind of tell you, and I think both are very valuable.

JDP: Where do you guys put Pynchon here on that spectrum? Is he showing or telling? I'd like to know, really.

JCO: Well, I think he's telling because it's all voice. It's performative, it's quite unique.

IM: It strikes me that the dictum to show not tell depends on the kind of consensus about what kinds of details one shows, which when put in front of the reader constitute a story, which means that you would have to have some kind of consensus among the readerly audience about what should be shown. That works if you're a white writer, or a writer who went through MFA program.

If you read Franzen, and he's really into showing, if you can recognize the cultural signals he's giving off, then that's a story for you. I read Franzen, and then I don't recognize anything in those novels that constitutes a story to me. I think like Joyce said, sometimes when you're telling a story from a marginalized or a different background, telling is necessary.

JDP: Can we get another question? Do we have time for a few more?

S1: [Speaker 1] Yeah, we have three people in line, if that's okay.

JDP: We'll stay forever.

S4: [Speaker 4] I was curious if you had any advice for people who are trying to break into the literary journals to build a name for themselves, as opposed to the online only, if that makes any sense, I hope.

JDP: Ismail works for *ZYZZYVA*, a terrific San Francisco–based national publication. There are booths everywhere throughout the Festival where magazines are featured, and I would say, take a look at the magazines. Find the stories and the poems that resonate for you, and that's a good place to seek publication.

IM: I would also say, that's something I learned just getting involved with *ZYZZYVA*, is that since I'm actually reading what gets submitted to the journal, so few things that get submitted actually get published in the journal or even make it to the editors, going to parties, I think, is a much better strategy than submitting … literally going to parties, meeting people, meeting editors and other writers, making connections, that's what's worked for me, and I think it's what's working for a lot of young emerging writers.

I feel like the literary journal submission thing is kind of a trap, I don't know.

JDP: You didn't come here for social tips, but there you go. We have time for a couple more, maybe.

S5: [Speaker 5] Hi, this is for you, Joyce. Your ability to get into characters' brains amazes me. On top of that, your characters get into my brain, and they stay, and they live there. I think about people that I've read in your books a lot, and I've read a lot of books. Your characters live in my brain. It's amazing.

My question is, do you have a muse? How do you do this superhuman feat?

JCO: Well, thank you for your remark. I don't think of it as superhuman. I spend a lot of time thinking about the characters, and sort of inhabiting them. I like to go for long walks, or even running, and just thinking about the work, not necessarily thinking about the writing of it, but more like thinking of the actual people. They start to live for me for quite a while before I write about them. It's like an aura or a feeling of almost like identification.

JDP: Thank you. That's been our panel about how stories make the world. I think we've completely covered that subject-

SS: Well, I think we have time for one more question.

S6: Thank you. I promise to be brief. I just wanted to ask, and I've been dying to ask this question for five years, because I know Joyce Carol Oates has the work with the World Science Festival, and I know Ismail was talking about his technology and this idea of science, and how science may invade your work. I wanted to hear more about that.

JCO: The question was about science and literature?

Well, it's such a complicated question. Probably in the last eight years or so, I've been much more aware of the world of science. I've been reading a lot of books on science and biographies, and thinking about the world, not so much from my earlier perspective, the writerly perspective, but rather more like an objective.

Science is based upon an evolution of ideas, so there's always a drama and excitement of new ideas and the world being transformed. Definitely, I've actually written about scientists, which I would not have done before.

JDP: We both admire *Version Control*, which is a terrific novel.

JCO: Dexter Palmer. He's an unclassifiable writer, isn't he?

JDP: Yeah.

AM: I think you asked how technology invades your work. I think that technology, aside from the discussion of it in broader social or cultural context, just purely as in nuts and bolts narrative issue, it presents a lot of hurdles for writers.

For instance, cell phones…having a cell phone in a novel, having two cell phones in a novel basically reduces a lot of dramatic choices. As soon as you have characters who can text each other, or call each other, or as soon as everybody in a fictional world knows where everybody else is, you lose a lot of opportunities for creating dramatic obstacles.

Think of how many books would have been solved on the first page if one character could just call another.

JCO: I solved that problem by having the phone run out of power.

AM: I'm going to steal that trick from you.

JDP: I want to acknowledge again UC Berkeley Arts and Design and the Simpson Family Literary Project. Thank you all for coming. We have authors' books in the lobby. And my very distinguished panel, Scott Saul, Ismail Muhammad, Anthony Marra, and Joyce Carol Oates. Thank you, have a wonderful day.

CORTÉS THE KILLER

BY SAMANTHA HUNT

2018 SIMPSON PRIZE FINALIST

It's starting to get dark. Beatrice walks the highway's shoulder from the bus depot to her family's house. She stays just outside the guardrail on the dry grass strewn with trash, matted down by road salt and rain. There's the bloated body of a dead raccoon. Beatrice is sure that every car and truck passing holds someone she knew in high school. Inside their cars they ask, "Is that Beatrice? What is she doing with a raccoon carcass?"

She turns up the drive. She hasn't seen the farm in more than a year. After her father died she moved away to the city—not for any good reason, but now she likes it there because the humiliations of entering her thirties as a single woman happen behind a closed apartment door, out of the view of her family and everyone she's ever known.

There are some weathered plastic Easter decorations wired to the front porch, a hip-high bunny rabbit and a bright green egg purchased at the drugstore. It is Thanksgiving. In the time she's been gone redneck clones of her brother and her mother have had their perverted redneck way with the house.

The farm is an island in a sea of big chain stores. While the surrounding farms were plowed under one by one and turned into shopping centers, her parents had stood by. They had waited rather than selling as the neighbors all had. They had waited with the thought, *Maybe this will stop, maybe the farms will return.* Now, along a ten-mile strip of parking lots, stores, gas stations, banks, and supermarkets, their farm is the only one left.

It isn't even much of a farm. Beatrice's parents gave up farming seven years before when, one morning, Beatrice's mother told her father, "I don't feel like getting out of bed." He looked her over and, holding her jaw in his hands, he studied her face for a long while before saying, "Yeah. I can see it. Right there on your forehead," as if there were a word written across her brow that excused her from farmwork for the rest of her life.

Within a few weeks Beatrice's father had become an expert crossword puzzle solver. He'd even considered writing a novel before realizing that soon they would be broke. Beatrice's parents had to start working or sell the farm. So they leased their land out to a conglomerate soybean operation and applied for jobs in the new industrial park. Her father found work as a loan adjuster, her mother a job in advertising, working in the satellite office of a company called Mythologic Development, where they turn myths and sometimes history into marketable packages used for making new products and ideas more digestible to the consumer public. Her father didn't like having an office job. He used his sick days as soon as he got them, but Beatrice's mother had always been very dramatic, someone who would swoon or leap without provocation; the sort of person who would sing while grocery shopping and then wonder why people were staring at her. She flourished during the brainstorming conference calls that were a regular feature of her new job. She'd dominate the conversations with her patched-together notions of Leda and the Swan, the void of Ginnungagap, the bubonic plague, and Hathor the Egyptian goddess, whom she reenvisioned as a nineteen-year-old Ukrainian supermodel spokesperson for a vodka company.

Beatrice's parents hadn't been born farmers. It was just one of many bright ideas they'd developed in their twenties, ideas like dropping out of college in their junior year, forgoing regular dentist visits, and having children they decided to name Beatrice and Clement.

"Right," Clem says after Thanksgiving dinner, standing to leave the table. He shakes his head at his mother, at Beatrice. Clem works as a carpenter, though he's mostly interested in small projects, cabinets and decks, hand-carving the names of rock bands into soft pieces of wood.

"Going to toke up?" Beatrice's mother asks him. He pops his head back inside the kitchen. He is stocky and solid like a bolted zucchini that has grown too long. He holds a finger and thumb up to his lips and inhales, pinching together a vacancy in between them.

Their mother has put a feather in her hair for the holiday, her "Indian headdress." She can't stand it that her youngest son is a pothead and sometimes she'll get a look, as if she's trying not to cry just thinking about it. She's a very good actress. She stares at Clem. He looks just like her, dark hair, red skin, and papery lips. Beatrice's mother can make her bottom jaw tremble so slightly that the movement is barely perceptible. She stares at him with her mouth wide open, waiting for him to feel guilty. Beatrice looks away. It is difficult for Beatrice to think of her mother as someone with thoughts and desires, as someone who keeps a vibrator in her bedside drawer the way Beatrice does, as someone who might dream about a tremendous ice cube, the size of a sofa, melting in the middle of a hot desert, and wake up having absolutely no idea what the dream means.

"Dude, I'm so stoned." Clem laughs once, faking a stumble before disappearing. As he opens the front door the flat sound of road traffic sneaks inside. Beatrice clears the table. She holds the turkey over the garbage by its breastbone, dangling it there while her mother splits what is left in the last wine bottle between their two glasses.

"When Atlantis was sinking there was an awful period of…" and Beatrice's mother stops to think of the proper word but can't. "Of sinking," she says and places her open hands on either side of her face, like the sunshine. Beatrice cringes at the gesture. Her mother is going to try to tell her something she doesn't want to hear. Her mother still works for Mythologic and believes all concepts are better communicated through specious retellings of ancient myths. Most of the time, Beatrice can't see the connections.

"Imagine," her mother says, her hands still in place. "People went to sleep inland and woke up with the ocean at their doors. When they stepped outside in the morning to pee or to feed their goats the neighbors were gone and the only sound was waves lapping."

Her mother slowly drags one finger across their kitchen table and then does it again. Beatrice remains entirely still, frozen like a field rabbit, hoping her mother will decide not to tell her whatever it is she wants to say. She can already imagine its perimeters: "Honey, I wish you would think about a job that offers insurance," or "I know a real nice young man you might like to meet, Bea." But he wouldn't be a nice young man.

He would be another forty-five-year-old divorced actor her mother had met through community theater projects, a man who also holds his hands up around either side of his face like the sunshine when he wants to make a point.

Or maybe she wants to tell Beatrice that she is finally going to sell the farm.

But Beatrice is wrong.

"When your dad was in the hospital the doctor gave me a choice, Bea." She rubs her palms across her skinny thighs, exhaling. "The doctor asked, 'Do you want to stop his pain?' And at first I said, yeah, of course, but then the doctor asked again, 'No. Do you really, really want to stop his pain?' And, Bea, I knew what he meant and I said yes. I killed your dad."

She is drunk.

"Oh. So *you* killed him?"

"Well, not me, but the doctor. I told the doctor to go ahead and get it over with."

"What does that have to do with Atlantis?" Beatrice asks.

Her mother has to think for a moment. She looks up at the ceiling. "We all have to die sometime?"

Beatrice stares straight ahead like a TV stuck on static, the remote control gone dead. She blinks a series of gray and black squiggled lines. No reception. Nothing. Her mother's words are not getting through; they are stones dropped into a bottomless hole, the hollow known as Beatrice. They fall and fall until they are too far away to be heard.

There's an unwound egg timer beside the stove. "You want to watch a movie, hon?" Static clears, program resumes. It's a story about a mother and her kids on a farm in Pennsylvania, a dull after-school special broadcast for the Thanksgiving holiday.

If Beatrice sits in the living room with her mother watching a movie, she'll explode—a dark green syrup of boredom her mother will have to sponge off the floor with Fantastik and a towel. "I'm going to go see what Clem's up to." Beatrice is still holding the turkey by its breastbone. It has started to sway. Beatrice drops the bird. It makes a swoosh, a rush of flight as it falls into the garbage bag.

When Beatrice was a girl, Clement still a baby, and the farm was in okay shape, Bea and her father walked the fields once a day. The furrows were dry and bulging and Beatrice liked how it felt when the dirt broke underneath her muck boots. Corn plants made a canopy over her head. She'd lose sight of everything except her father's legs marching ahead of her. She'd put her hand inside his and he'd hold it roughly as if her hand was a mouse he'd captured. She'd pretend he was not her father at all but a boyfriend, someone from TV.

He said: "Don't tell your mom, but I'm the king of the farmers." They walked on a bit farther and came across an irrigation hose that had cracked its rubber tubing. Her father fingered the leak and stared out at the land with every intention of coming back and patching up the cracked hose. He'd never come back. He just liked to look that way from time to time.

"Farming," he'd say, "takes ten percent perspiration and ninety percent inspiration." Beatrice had heard this the other way around, but didn't let on. Maybe he was the king. He wasn't a bad farmer. He just didn't do things the way they had always been done. For instance, pruning trees—he had no time for it, or thinning plants. He hated to yank up seedlings that had been eager enough to sprout. He'd let the vegetables grow on top of one another. He'd let the carrots and beets twist around each other, deformed by proximity. "They still taste as sweet," he'd say, but no one wanted to buy the bent oddities that came from such close growing quarters.

Beatrice's father rarely wore proper farmer clothing. Instead he dressed in chinos, button-down oxford shirts, and canvas sneakers. "They're cheap" is all he ever had to say. He looked like James Dean in the movie *East of Eden*. James Dean on a John Deere. He'd hay the fields, and Beatrice would follow behind in the trail of the tractor's exhaust, so it would be hard for her to know what was an act and what was real.

Sodium vapor lamps from the mall parking lots wash away any definition for miles around. Everything on the farm glows the same yellow gray at night. Beatrice trips on a pig trough her mother's been using as a planter for impatiens.

"What's up, dude?" her brother asks when she yelps. Clem has converted half of the barn into an apartment. She stumbles in. There are no locks on his apartment because his door is an old cellar hatch taken off a house demolished to make way for a Dunkin' Donuts. His kitchen countertops are built from plywood the Home Depot used as concrete molds and then tossed. Most of his apartment is built from stuff he lifted off construction sites. It's a common practice among Clem's friends because they can't yet not own the land they've always owned. "Matthew Campbell's milking pavilion used to be here, so I guess we can just help ourselves."

"Let's go downtown," Beatrice says. "See if the stores are open on Thanksgiving."

"I guess." Clem's uncertain about going out in the cold, but still enough under the sway of his older sister that he'll do what she wants to do. He detaches himself from his video game.

"Can I try that first?" she asks.

"This?" He holds the controller up. "Yeah, yeah sure." He restarts the game. "Do you know how to play?"

"No."

"I'll start you off slowly." He slips her hand into a glove that is rigged with controls. It is filled with tiny nodes like suction cups, the dead raccoon's puckered skin. "Sit down," he says, and she does.

At first nothing happens. The screen turns blue and the nodes tickle her hand. Clem fusses with the machinery.

The apartment is tiny and the walls are mostly covered with shelves and cabinets. Clem moved out of the main house when he fell in love with Anna. They moved into the barn together after high school and lived here for almost five years. But Anna moved away to the city a year ago. She hasn't picked up all her stuff yet. Clothes, some textbooks that she and Clem kept from school, and a nice set of silver that Anna's grandparents gave her. Everything is covered with bits of old hay from the barn. Sometimes Anna and Beatrice meet up for coffee in the city. They never talk about the farm or Clem. They act like survivors from a low-budget, straight-to-DVD apocalypse.

The video game starts up. A woman walks through a Zen Buddhist garden, wearing a tight silver outfit, carrying a long sword.

"That's you. Use the glove to go forward."

Beatrice walks slowly through the garden, because someone is going to tiptoe up behind her, a horrible machete, and she's had a number of glasses of red wine. She's not sure she can fight back. Beatrice feels the girl walk, inside the girl's digital skin.

Clem lights a joint and hums the video game's theme, a soundtrack. The girl on the screen creeps forward, flashes the blade of her sword. Beatrice accepts the joint with her ungloved hand, jerking the controls. The girl on-screen stands still, doing nothing, flicking her sword, walks backward, looks toward the couch. Beatrice holds the smoke in her lungs long enough for both of them.

There are pathways to the left and the right in the garden. Beatrice can't turn yet. Clem hums the tune. Beatrice exhales, imagining a man with a deep radio voice speaking over the music, whispering into Beatrice's ear, reading her the fine print. It fills her with longing just the same.

A pack of ninja warriors surprises her from above, and after a very short fight Beatrice is dead.

It is colder than most Thanksgivings. The ruts in the driveway have solidified, forming seals of creaky ice. Beatrice and Clem walk to his truck in silence. She still feels as if she's on-screen with the video game's sharpened abilities. She controls the world with her hand, senses sounds with her skin, hears her brother's fingers jangle the keys in his pocket. She hears her mother sigh as the mid-movie commercial break starts. Beatrice hasn't smoked pot in a long time. She feels every person who has ever stepped on the driveway. Oil deliverymen. Tractor repairmen. Lenape Indians. She feels the outline of these people precisely, solid bodies beneath her feet. She squishes faces with her boots.

Beatrice has an idea. "Let's take Humbletonian," she says, letting go of the truck's door handle. Humbletonian is a horse. When her parents sold the farm animals they kept a few chickens for eggs and one horse named Humbletonian. Her father named the horse this because she was not a Hambletonian. A Hambletonian is a very distinguished trotting horse. A Humbletonian is nothing. It is like changing your name to Stonerfeller because you are not a Rockefeller.

"In the trailer?" her brother asks, and then answers the question himself. "No. Ride the horse into town? Right? Right. Cool," he says, eyes glassy. They walk back to the barn, breaking ice again.

After their father stopped farming he sometimes took a sleeping bag to the loft above the horse's stable after dinner. He'd smoke cigarettes up there and spend the night like a Boy Scout. He thought that the horse's wild nature could make him feel better about working in an office. He thought the horse could soothe the unease in his rib cage. From the loft her father pretended he was Jerry Lee Lewis, an old table saw platform for the piano. He'd sing to the horse. "You. Leave. Me." Pause. Pause. "Breathless." Though her father's odd behavior seemed exciting at the time, Beatrice now thinks that horses aren't wild. Horses can't soothe our unease in the world. Horses are about the most broken, unwild creatures in existence, except for maybe burros and dogs. They do exactly what humans tell them to do. So when she thinks now how her father slept in the barn, rode Humbletonian across their forty acres because he thought it would cure the unease in his chest, it only makes her sad. That wasn't unease, Dad. It was lung cancer.

"Hello, pumpkin pie." Clem pets Humbletonian's nose. The barn smells yellow—urine and old pine boards.

The horse's belly sags in a way that reminds Beatrice of a velour reclining chair. "Hello, La-Z-Boy girl." Beatrice kisses the horse. Humbletonian does not look particularly happy to see her. Clem attaches bit and bridle. He puts a hand on the saddle straddling the stable wall, but Beatrice shakes her head no. Clem leads the horse outside by the reins and crouches down on one knee, keeping the other lifted square. Beatrice uses Clem's knee as a boost and climbs up onto the horse's bare back. "Whoop," Beatrice whoops. In a moment her brother is seated behind her. Clem wraps big zucchini arms around her sides, reaching for the reins.

Brother and sister are quiet as they trot through harvested fields. The sound of dead stalks and frost crunching under Humbletonian's hooves fills the gray quiet of the night. The video game's theme rattles in the back of Beatrice's head.

"I don't know what she'll think of the road," Clem says. "I don't think she's ever been past the far field." Their mother only uses the horse when her car gets stuck in the muddy divots of their driveway. She harnesses Humbletonian to the bumper, pulling while she pushes.

They reach the end of the driveway. Humbletonian turns left and trots along the breakdown lane, as if she can't wait to get down to town, as if there's nothing to it.

On the road Humbletonian's hooves sound like winter—metal on ice or an empty galvanized pail tossed down a stone staircase. They pass an abandoned barn that is wedged between two service stations and two narrow swaths of dried red clover. Someone has spray-painted the words LUV SHAK below a tin sign advertising the Crystal Cave tourist attraction. The land is flat and open here. The road is the straightest road there is. It runs all the way down to where the Pennsylvania Dutch people live in villages named Blue Ball, Intercourse, Paradise.

An eighteen-wheeled tanker whooshes past Humbletonian. It blows Beatrice's body to the right. A car honks before passing. The man in the backseat does not seem surprised to see a horse and riders on the highway on Thanksgiving evening. He throws his cigarette butt toward them so it explodes against the asphalt, a bomb sized for insects.

"I'm going to puke," she says.

"No. No, you won't." Clem pats her on the back one, two, three times. Beatrice leans against Humbletonian's neck. The warmth of the horse on her stomach. They ride the rest of the way in silence except for the click of Humbletonian's hooves and the rush of the horse's warm pulse.

One of the myths Beatrice's mother was responsible for developing was a fictionalized version of Montezuma meeting Cortés for the first time. Her mother's coworkers rarely bothered to differentiate between those things that had actually happened and those things that people just used to say had happened. They'd take history and add to it and no one knew the difference anymore. For example, they might say that Montezuma could fly through the air carrying three virgins at a time to a sacrificial altar in the sky. They might say that there was bloodshed when these two men met or that Cortés was part man, part horse.

Mythologic Development sold the Montezuma-Cortés myth to an amusement park in Maryland, which used it for a roller coaster called the Aztecathon. The concept sold for a good price, but her mother was a salaried employee and so she saw very little of the money. Now the amusement park owns Montezuma. He is their intellectual property.

Beatrice's mother keeps a painting of Montezuma over her bed. In the painting he looks more like a famous movie star than like an Aztec ruler. Beatrice's mother likes that about him. She tells Beatrice that she is in love with Montezuma now that Beatrice's father is gone.

"Montezuma's also dead," Beatrice says, and her mother smiles as if that were a really good joke.

"Who-ah." Humbletonian turns into the Middleland Mall Complex. They pass through a large empty lot dotted with circles of light. It is freezing cold. "Who-ah." Humbletonian clops to a halt outside the Walmart entrance. At the doors, they wait on the horse. Their breath is visible in the cold air. Humbletonian stomps her hoof as though asking, "What next?" Her motion is detected by a sensor. The door swings open to let them in. Humbletonian takes a few steps back before she steadies.

They'd have to duck their heads to make it through the entry. "I bet they've never had a horse inside there." Clem tilts his neck. A security officer stationed by the theft-deterrent column stands to adjust his utility belt. He eyes their transportation with more than suspicion. He steps outside.

"I know you're not even thinking about bringing that beast in here," he says.

"But I *was* thinking of it," Clem says. "So you're wrong."

The guard palms his nightstick. He looks like just the sort of security officer who would have Clem ticketed for an inane livestock violation still on the books from 1823. No Horse-Riding on Public Holidays. Clem slides off Humbletonian, leading Beatrice over to the corral for collecting shopping carts. He ties Humbletonian's reins to the metal bar. Beatrice slides off the curve of her flank.

Few people seem to be shopping. Clem asks a young man in a Walmart smock, "Excuse me. What's going on here?"

The young man raises his eyebrows, waiting for some clue as to how he can assist them. "Lots of things are going on here," the boy says finally.

"Walmart's open?" Clem asks. "It's Thanksgiving."

The boy stares at the dog food he's been pricing, looking to the back of the shelf, seeing something golden but invisible to everyone else.

Clem bends to see what the boy's looking at. Just the back of the metal shelf. Clem grabs Beatrice's arm and leads her away.

Up front, the store is ready for Christmas. Past Christmas comes an aisle of automotive and craft/hobby supplies, then an aisle of hair products and footwear, then an aisle of watches and diamond-chip rings. All of these aisles dead-end at the wall of sporting goods/hunting gear. Ladies' and menswear are intersected by a row of birthday cards, logic-puzzle books, scented candles, deodorant, and toothpaste. Beatrice and Clem pass the electronics division. They're sold out of the game Clem was thinking about buying, Dead or Alive 5000. There is a paper SALE sign that Clem swipes at.

"Do you need anything?"

Beatrice detects a flashing pulse in the fluorescent lighting. "Nope. Let's go."

Clem takes a pack of gum, puts it in his pocket. "For Mom," and they leave quickly without paying for the gum.

Outside, Humbletonian is no longer tied up. She is gone, and Beatrice bets it was the security guard. "Shit." Clem giggles because, by the shopping-cart corral, there is a pile of horseshit that Humbletonian left behind.

Clem scans the parking lot. The circles of light underneath each lamp are still there, but no horse. "You go that way," Clem tells Beatrice. "I'll go this way and I'll meet you around back. We'll flush her out." Clem departs around one side of the giant complex and Beatrice walks off in the other direction.

The store is so long that she feels as though she'll never even reach the corner of it. Beatrice is an astronaut dragging a two-hundred-pound space suit. That's why her footsteps can't carry her forward. She stops altogether. "I wouldn't have killed him," Beatrice says out loud. She waits until she hears a question from the far side of her brain, from her mother. "What would you have done? Just let him suffer? Let him go on breathing that bubbly wet breath that sounded like a damn water fountain?"

"Yes," Beatrice answers. "Yes, I would have."

The Walmart does not end. It goes on and on, windowless and solid. Beatrice thinks of the old cartoons. An illustrator draws two panels of background, a desert or a pine forest, and by bringing one panel in front of the other, he can keep it going forever, a duplicated landscape Wile E. Coyote can run through. If she had four legs like Humbletonian she'd be able to get around the back of the mall faster. She thinks to skip but after ten or eleven lengths her lungs chug and backfire on the cold air. She walks the rest of the way.

Behind the shopping center there are bulldozers, at least twenty of them huddled with their backs to Beatrice, in a private conference. It's freezing. Apart from the dozers there's nothing here except a gigantic hole. It is tremendous, far larger than a football field, and it is filled with water. In the dark, the hole extends beyond the limit of Beatrice's vision. Clem is already standing at the edge, looking down into it. Humbletonian is there, too. She has climbed down into the pit and is walking across the surface of the ice formed there. It's like a lake. Maybe one of the bulldozers broke a water pipe while digging. There's a lot of water here, a reservoir's worth, or, Beatrice hopes not, frozen sewage. Humbletonian is walking across the ice, bending every now and again to lick the surface.

"Woo-hoo! Humbletonian!" Clem yells. "Good horse. Good horse," he shouts. Humbletonian turns from where she is, halfway across the ice, and when she sees Clem and Beatrice she begins to trot across the very center of the pit toward them, more like a dog than a horse. Her coat is as silver as the ice, and beautiful.

Beatrice lifts up her arms and shakes her hips. "Woo-hoo! Horsey!" she calls. Time slows to a pace where Beatrice can notice every single thing. Humbletonian's muscles, her breath coming out of her flared nostrils, and the odd rhythm of her trot. She notices the gorgeous ice and dirt and the lovely darkness, thick as felt, existing in this ugly place. She can hear each hoof as it falls against the ice. Beauty stands nearby, a shadowy person whose exhales become Beatrice's inhales, warming her up, and this moment of warmth, this beautiful horse, is why a jealous hole cracks open in the ice, swallowing the back legs and hindquarters of Humbletonian faster than thought.

Humbletonian tries to clear the water, to get a hoof back up on solid ice, but each clop of her front hooves shatters what she's grabbed. There can't be that much water underneath her. But there is. She's not touching the bottom. Humbletonian flails. Clem starts to swear, but slowly; everything is happening so slowly at first that time will come to a halt and the world behind the shopping center will be all right. It might even be possible to ignore the drowning horse altogether. Beatrice and her brother are here only in a dream. They will both wake up soon.

Beatrice reaches her arms even higher. "Clem," she says. Clem wrings his hands. He lowers himself into the pit, down to where the ice starts. He is moving slowly, carefully. Humbletonian is thrashing. It's the only sound. The water must be freezing. "Clem," Beatrice says again, and again Clem wrings his hands so hard he might tear them off by his wrists. He steps out onto the edge of the ice and creeps toward Humbletonian. She is in up to her middle. Only her front hooves and her head are above the ice. Clem stops. The horse is twisting and snorting. She screams as much as a horse can scream. Clem raises his hands to his face. He takes another step toward the horse. "Clem," Beatrice repeats his name a third time. He turns to look at her. A seam has been cut open in Clem through the center of his face. A seam that says there is no way to stop this. No way for a man to save a horse drowning in freezing water. Clem stands still. He brings his hands up to his ears and, pressing the small knobs of cartilage there, he stops listening.

Quiet moments pass. The static returns, as though it were being broadcast from nearby. Humbletonian starts giving up. She falls still. The water has dropped her into shock. Beatrice can see a lot of white in the horse's eye, as though it had been pried open. It blinks dry air once more, for the last time. Humbletonian's head goes under. Her forelegs, above the barrier of the ice, kick, emptying what's inside them. It is a gruesome convulsion.

"She's getting away." Beatrice skids on her heels down to where her brother stands. She walks out onto the ice. A loud crack bellows from the frozen water, like a whip pushing Beatrice back, away from her horse. Beatrice drops to her knees on the ice and Humbletonian goes under all the way. Their horse is gone. The water flattens out over her head.

Clem lowers his hands. "Don't." But Beatrice doesn't listen. She sits down on the ice and watches the hole where Humbletonian went. She slides closer toward it on her knees. The hole doesn't do anything.

The silence fills in around Beatrice and Clem like insulation. The two of them look down into the black hole where their horse disappeared, waiting, maybe, for some triumphant geyser, a phoenix, or Pegasus to rise up out of the hole. Fifteen minutes pass, maybe half an hour before they recognize what they are staring at: an empty black hole.

"Clem." Beatrice has her back still turned to him, still looking at the hole. "You know what Mom told me?"

"What?"

"She gave the doctor permission to kill Dad."

"Yeah, I know," Clem says.

"You know?"

"She asked me what I thought before she did it."

No one asked Beatrice. She sat by her father's hospital bed for days, rubbing lotion into the dry skin of his calves and feet, and no one said anything to her. "No one asked me."

"We already knew what you'd say."

Since her father's death, Beatrice's parents have been two-dimensional pieces of paper she folds up, tucks into her back pocket, and forgets about when she does her laundry, fishing them out of the lint trap later: her mother all things bad, her father all things good. But Clem ruins it every time. There's Clem, sitting on the ice, shaking his head, saying, "It's no one's fault, Bea." But Beatrice would like to find someone to blame.

Even with the static, she sees a map in front of her, a map of yesterday, today, and tomorrow. She sees that they arrived here at this future rather than a different one. One with horses. Maybe that future would have been better. But they had arrived here to a time when their farm is dead, when Beatrice has moved away to the city, when Clem is stuck in place, and when, most nights, her mother walks down to the end of the driveway, out to meet the incoming tide in Pennsylvania.

Beatrice leans forward, lowering her whole body onto the ice. She pushes herself on her stomach out to where the horse disappeared. She lies there. She rests her cheek there for a long time. She pets her horse through the ice. "Don't go any farther," Clem says. Beatrice dips her hand inside the hole, into a land that is already lost.

REVIVAL GIRL

BY MARTIN POUSSON

2018 SIMPSON PRIZE FINALIST

Under the fluorescent glare of the kitchen, Mama sang a gospel tune and shelved groceries to an imaginary beat. Each can, bottle, and box faced forward, like votive offerings. Lined in straight rows, the pantry rack collected a religious order, only missing gold leaf and stained glass. Food was hallowed in Louisiana, its magic put to work in all manner of faiths. Not just herbs for hexes but roots, leaves, seeds, bones, and skins. Spells, cures, omens, all called for some piece of a plant or part of an animal that might also land on a dinner plate. If you wanted to quell the nerves, you stuffed a bag with the hairy flower of frog-foot. If you wanted to hinder the heart, you stewed the hooked fruit of devil's claw. And if you wanted to predict the sex of a baby, you swung a meaty tailbone over the pregnant belly. A steady swing meant a boy, a gyrating swing meant a girl, and an in-between swing meant a third kind of baby, the kind no one wanted to name.

There I stood in Mama's tall shadow, the no-name kind of baby. The light from the fridge radiated a halo around her dark cloud of hair. A carton of eggs glowed in her hand. Her long legs shifted back and forth, like a crane at dawn. Even though she tapped her heels to the song, I knew better than to tap along with her or, worse, to twirl across the linoleum flapping my hands in the air. By three, I'd learned penance for the jitters when Mama strapped down my restless hands with duct tape then ordered a doctor to fit braces on my twisting feet. By five, I'd learned sacrifice for the stutters when another doctor cut out a flap of flesh to correct my tangling speech. Mama showed me the horn-shaped piece to prove a point: the devil had me by the tongue. So I did my best to walk straight and talk steady.

Still, my feet pranced and my arms swung more than any boy Mama had known. At first glance, my body seemed drawn into the right shape, but my walk swished and swayed, and my hands flapped in the air or flitted at my side. A tremor in my chest pushed my ribs out when I grew anxious, as if I might burst. At times, I stared at a point between my eyes before boxing my ears with two fists or slapping my face with an open palm. Just what brewed inside me? Mama wondered. Just what made up my tailbone? Soon, she'd open that carton of eggs in her hand. Soon, she'd test that boy on the floor.

Cousins, blood relations, were the only boys Mama had known before marrying at sixteen. Short boys smelling of foul ditches, with loose tongues, rough hands, stiff lips, headed for the half-life of the oil patch. And the only man she knew, her towering father, had gone by the time she hit her teens, leaving her to tend two baby sisters and, as she put it, a baby mother. The girls made monstrous faces from the floor, crying for milk, syrup, toys, solace.

Her mother, my *mamère*, was an angry baby too, full grown, with three daughters and half a husband, but prone to pouting for days on end and pulling at her face until marks and stains rose on her skin. Jaundiced, with an odd yellow cast and a flame-red mark near her left eye, she frowned and winced and usually wore what the frosted-wig Cajun ladies called *le grimace*.

"That woman is marked," they said, while rubbing their hands over a set of rosary beads. As soon as they heard she was from Sulphur, they knew the cause. That place looked, smelled, and tasted yellow. Water streamed with colored bits, soil crumbled into colored chunks, and air choked with colored clouds. Oil derricks clotted the town like metal birds boring for food. Tanker trucks rocked the roads leaving a tail of exhaust fumes and a crest of mineral traces. Who could look at all that and see anything but the devil?

Mama had heard the legends about her mother's town and her father's cove, where Sabine men dug into the swampy ground with their own homemade drills and bits to raise houses on piers. Or else, they pushed off the land altogether to float in house boats on the Vermilion or the Teche, the phantom limbs of the Mississippi. Any oil drilled out of the ground, any minerals pumped into the air didn't belong to them.

They owned no land, only boats, no farms, only fishing nets. And they did their best to outrun the changing tides and shifting coast of the gulf.

A girl in that place was her own dowry. With sable-black hair and a body that swayed like a cattail reed, Mama could've had any Sabine man. The center of her irises flashed a speckled green and her skin flushed with a copper flame. She was true Cajun on one side, *la vraie chose*, but Sabine on the other, an odd mix of French, African, and a dying Indian tribe. The wolf-faced boys opened their mouths in a howl when she passed. But she wanted no half-life, no half-husband, no near-man. She wanted no floating home. So she sang to herself and waited for a boy from another town and the exit sign.

And what had she learned before she left the cove, before she married? That the devil lurked everywhere, in drinking water, in mud under your shoe, in the wrath and cholera of family. That faith had to be conjured, cooked up with a powerful hand. That women snapped at each other like crawfish in a boiling pot while men ran like horses through wide open fields.

Her father had galloped in and out the front door for years, sometimes with another woman at his side. He reared back, dropped her on the couch, then hollered into the kitchen for a tall girl. He laughed at his own joke, calling his tall daughter to bring him a tall can of beer. Mama got the joke but didn't laugh. She worried how he magically pulled a six-pack from a paper sack while she rationed lost bread for her sisters, spiked off milk with syrup, and shaved slices from the block of gray cheese. Yet if the bread, the milk, the cheese, and—yes—the beer rankled, her father's women impressed Mama with their light hair and light eyes and elevated him above their lot.

He was elevated in other ways too. As part-time minister in the church of the Pentecost, and as full-time voodoo *traiteur*, my *papère* soared even before his crane of a daughter. In a tent revival, he stood head and shoulders above the penitents when he walked the aisles waving the Holy Bible. He leaned over weeping women and called foreign words out of their mouth. He shouted down stooping men and pulled ailments out of their body. Throughout, he smiled wide, his forehead glistened and even the fillings in his teeth gleamed in testament to his word. Then at home, he raised his hand to the porch ceiling to hang black chickens, their guts dripping like yellow rain. From his seat on a wingback chair, he cured a baby's deadly whooping cough with a rabbit's belly and the milky sap of a tala tree. He ground up stinging nettle to make a gullet-scorching brew for a man who cheated him in cards. He burned onion skins for money and peanut shells for luck. He rubbed his hairy hand over a doll with a worried cross-stitched mouth while Mama's cousins collected at his feet and called him Chief.

Her father could work magic both ways, the white voodoo and the black. The rumor was, given some moolah, a shot, and a pair of dice, he could solve any predicament. He'd throw the numbers on the ground, slam the shot down his throat, then strut around like a rooster with his tail on fire until he finally slapped his hands together and shouted, "Sweet Jesus!"

And, like that, he could tell you in exactly what part of the woods to find a thirty-point buck or how to exhume a dead skunk from under your house with nothing but a chain of beer tabs, a fish hook, and a free hand. He knew from whose backyard to steal the best sassafras root, which herbs needed rubbing together to cure a child's croup, and how to boil chicken gizzards and bayou gum to induce an immobilizing pox or a severe case of the runs for whoever dared to cross you.

With shoulder-length hair, a hawk-like nose, and a chin so sharp it could work as a nutcracker, in her stories Mama's father was the one man who could hold the entire world, steady and straight. Once, he spun an egg in his hand before her very eyes without it ever falling or hitting the ground. With a single tap, the whole shell fell away like brittle candy and there stood the perfect egg.

Yet she also saw her father crack. She watched him heat up a spoon with black tar before sticking a needle into his skin. Or else, he rolled up tin foil and stuck a straw in a line of smoke. Soon she smelled it—the sulfur in the air—and with that whiff, she knew he'd become the other man. He might, with a single horse kick, put a hole through the bedroom door. He might run outside and send a fruit tree sailing through the front window. He might tear the whole house in two.

Just before she turned thirteen, Mama saw her father lifted in his wingback chair by a sheriff and two deputies. He refused to budge when they showed a summons, so they carried that chair off the porch and onto the lawn where they dumped him into a net. He let loose a howl as they slapped a pair of handcuffs on his wrist then laughed and shouted a streak of hot words in French. Her mother emerged from the bedroom, suddenly an old lemon-faced woman, crying that she had married a werewolf, while women in wigs stood at the edge of the ditch, clucking their tongues. The red lights flashed and the siren shrieked as they drove her father away.

Yet they couldn't drive him out of her mind. Her eyes saw him everywhere: in passing cars, in big-armed trees, in a waking dream. He stood onstage under a tent wide as a sugar cane field. His feet floated above the ground and his hand reached out to heal a congregation of writhing people all at once. A young girl sang at his back, a raucous number that made the tent shake from side to side. He slapped his hand on the Bible then turned up a palm with an egg in the center, a brilliant white. Then the dream flickered and went dark on a single dancing flame.

Within weeks, she found a tent, filled with rolling bodies and a tall minister hoisting the Good Book overhead. A girl was pulled onstage to sing lead on a gospel song. When the words left her mouth, the tent billowed and the poles buckled. "He's got the whole world in his hands," she sang, as if each syllable were followed by an exclamation mark. People lifted their heads to the sky, shook their lips open until words tore out, and yanked their own hair until their scalps bled. Those with shoes tossed them onto the stage and joined those without. Together, they dug their feet into the muddy soil making a greasy floor. In the middle of all that grease, they danced faster and faster, more and more furiously, sawing their legs in and out to the beat of the gospel song. Some ripped at a sleeve or a collar, others were left standing in their underwear before the minister shouted a foreign word and promised to drop them in the water. When she caught his eye, though, she saw a ring of yellow and knew his magic was phony. His smile was too tight, his forehead too dry, and his hands too small. That minister had none of her father's power, none of his fire or faith. No man did. Not any minister anywhere, not one of her cousins or uncles then, and not her husband now.

When she made her move out of the dark roux of the swamp, Mama headed for the light grain of the rice field. She traded the Pentecostal faith for the Catholic one. She donned a mantilla and gloves, gave up the week-long revivals, the robed choir, the stamping feet and overturned chairs, and even the language of tongues— all for a man with a job in another town and a car to drive her away. To her, away meant another world. It meant a new life. It meant the promise of anywhere but here.

Even so, she made a gumbo faith, a jambalaya religion. During Mass, she wondered at the mortification of the saints, the bloody Crucifixion of Christ, and the seven swords in the Mother of Sorrows. She endured the boredom of the liturgy and the drone of the homily. Yet at home, she turned on the AM radio to hear the storm of a gospel song break out in her ears, a chorus of voices rising in a ferocious wind, lifting her higher and higher, on a soaring bird, a galloping horse, carrying her further and further away.

The man she married—my father—had a dry forehead, like that phony minister, she said. Small hands and a small quiet chest too. He'd taken her no more than half an hour from the bayou cove and gave her no more than half a house. A duplex apartment with plastic counters, plastic floors, and plastic lights overhead. It was brick, she had to admit, not cinder block. And the walls weren't stuffed with *bousillage*. But still she wanted out.

Her mind rattled with maps and compasses and a spinning wheel of direction. Her ears echoed with the hum of old women and old stories. Her eyes burned with flaming creatures and the yellow sign of a dead-end. And now in the altar of the kitchen, she wanted to know: could I deliver? Could I direct her out of here?

Mama raised her hand to testify, playing minister, choir, and congregation all at once. She sang louder and higher than the radio, her voice rocking the air around us until it shook like a thunder cloud. Half the words drowned under the raining clap of her hands, while the other half tore out in a lightning flash.

"You and me, brother, in his hands!"

Clap, clap!

"You and me, sister, in his hands!"

Clap, clap!

At the end of each verse, she twirled around to stare at me on the floor, checking to see if I was still there or if I'd tipped over into a place she couldn't reach. While she sang, her long finger pointed down at my head then made jabs in the air around her. I followed that finger and must've struggled to figure out the meaning of her dance. Each wave of her arm, each blink of her eye, each clap of her hands revealed another mystery, dark and cryptic. Soon something would crack. I'd move my mouth, my arms, or my legs in the wrong way. Soon, I'd end up sitting in another doctor's office or kneeling on the kitchen floor with hands taped to my chest.

Instead, Mama opened the carton of eggs, took one out and placed it in my hand. She looked straight into my eyes, as if she could see affirmation, a prayer or votive. Then she balanced the egg in the middle of my palm, upside down on its northern point and—for a long moment—it spun in a perfect orbit.

In the *Golden Book* stories Mama read at night, the cherubic altar boy would've carried that egg—proud and high, sure and steady—like an alabaster tooth from the mouth of God. But the devil boy would've bared his own yellow teeth, would've shaken the egg and sucked the yolk right out of the shell. Which was I, Mama wanted to know, cherub or devil? What was I, a steady boy or another kind?

"Hold it," she said, "hold it."

Her eyes grew wide and glowed like green marbles. Here was her hope. Here was her way out of this cramped house, with its belljar rooms and matchbox furniture. Here was her toddler listening to her command. She'd done right to read proper English to me, to forbid anyone to speak Cajun gibberish over my crib. She'd done right to show me how to genuflect, how to bow, how to button a shirt, how to clean under my nails, how to stay out of the sun, how to keep my face white, how to be a real man, not a wild little Sabine beast.

"Hold it," she said, "hold it."

It was a whole world, that egg. Now it spun in my hand. And as long as Mama gazed at me, it kept spinning. Before her magic-making eyes, I became the cherub and performed another wondrous miracle. Her baby who walked before his first birthday and talked before he walked, her boy who lined up all his toys in straight rows, her son who just the night before sat upright in his bed sleep-talking from Holy Scripture, this son of hers was now carrying the world she placed in his hands. He was now performing the same magic as her lost father, that minister and traiteur.

"Hold it," she said, "Hold it as long as you can."

Before her eyes and mine, the egg began to spin out of control in a shaky orbit. It was a simple command, just a couple of words, but I couldn't get it right, couldn't keep it straight. I should've known how to hold it, like her folklore father, how to control the world she gave me. But the wobbly sphere in my hand turned round and round, and my eyes crossed as it spun faster and faster, more and more furiously until it looked like a storm in my palm, the tiny white eye of a hurricane.

Then my fingers twitched, my palm shook, a storm broke out, and the whole world went spinning. The egg flew from my hand to the floor, setting off a display of yolky lightning along the way. Mama's newly mopped floor, the bleached tiles, the white cabinets, her gleaming patent leather shoes, and the trim of her skirt were all coated in yellow sticky ooze. Though I'd dropped only one egg, it looked as if a dozen brilliant suns had burst all around us. I stared at Mama, and she stared at me, until the nerves in my legs began to buckle. I slapped down my palm, trying to numb the pulsing sensation. But when Mama's long finger pointed at me, a warm, yellow trickle ran down my leg and collected in a puddle at my bare feet. In a flash, I plunged my hands down my pants to squeeze off the problem.

And that's when it all finally cracked. Mama took a good hard look at me and suddenly saw the devil before her. She'd somehow missed it all along, how she'd given birth not to a perfect Cajun son, not to a Catholic altar boy, but to bayou spawn, a pant-wetting, egg-dropping son of Satan.

"What in the Hell!" she kept screaming, her eyes wide and wild. "What in the sulfur-reeking, flame-licking, burning name of Hell are you doing with your hands in your pants?"

"Holding it," I said.

"Holding it!" she screamed.

My answer and her echo sent Mama running for the fridge. When she turned back around, she glowed the way she would in a dream, and I could no longer say what was true and what was not. I had dropped an egg. That much was certain. I had broken my mother's heart with a weak small hand. That was certain too. Yet was she singing that song? Was she clapping like mad?

When I looked up, Mama had turned into a red-eyed furious little girl staring down a jittery phantom. In one hand she held the carton of eggs, with the lid flipped open, and in the other she was cradling a phosphorescent white oval in her palm. She didn't place this one in my hand, though. Instead, she flung it to the ground. Then she flung another egg at the cabinet. Suddenly eggs were flying everywhere— at the sink, the stove, the baseboard. At the walls, the floor, the countertop. Mostly, though, at me. Egg ran down my face and arms and into my mouth before the carton was empty, the kitchen was coated yellow, and she finally stopped.

Tears ran down Mama's dream face in little rivers, then they ran down mine too. Along with the eggs, my mouth became a sea of grainy salt and slimy sulfur.

Yet the revival wasn't over. Mama dragged me across the kitchen to the concrete floor of the pantry where she planted me on two skinny knees. Lord knows her son had made a mess. Lord knows how badly she wanted me to get it right, to be the good cherub. And everyone knows a revival's not over until someone is stricken by the spirit, accused of some unholy crime, and made to confess. Eyes cross, tongues thicken, and whole bodies go rolling into the aisle. I kneeled and begged forgiveness, while a string of Blessed Be's and Hallowed Names crossed my mother's lips and she chased herself around the room, shouting as if her hair had been singed and her feet were on fire.

Finally, she dragged me to the closet in my bedroom and shut the door. Between the slats, I could see her tall slim figure pacing back and forth in front of my bed. And before her shadow slipped out of view, I heard one voice, then two, rising high and loud, singing the song from the kitchen and clapping to the beat of a pair of heels.

"You and me, brother, in His hands!"

Clap, clap!

"You and me, sister, in His hands!"

Clap, clap!

In the darkness, I bit my arm until I raised a red bump. I bit long and hard until I could no longer hear the sound of those two divided voices. The falling voice of a woman dropping something precious from her hand, and the rising voice of a girl watching in horror as it hit the ground. The low raging thunder of the words, and the high crying rain of the song.

"The itty bitty baby in His hands!

He's got the whole world in His hands!"

Oh, but where are the soaring horses now, Mama? Where are all the men?

Who will be there when the storm breaks, when the hand drops, when the Pentecost falls?

POEMS

BY GEOFFREY O'BRIEN

SIMPSON PROJECT COMMITTEE

FOUR LAST SONS
(FROM *PEOPLE ON SUNDAY*)

The sound was like picking sad battles,
The red that white imagines yellow is.

It was the sound of forgetting what
To do with the senses, being equally

Surprised by a voice subsiding, come
Slowly back, or edging toward actual close.

I'd forgotten to pay attention for years
To a song I heard for the first time

At the end of a recent memorial,
An actual song by Strauss about going

To sleep, predicting one's own death, etc.
Let me say this: I was surprised it kept

Going then surprised that it ended.
This was always true but could be more so

Much like those years of not knowing
The song felt brought back now

As inattention to its presence then.
And there are many versions

Of *Four Last Songs* and of this one,
As many as there are people

Who've made and played them.
Each one stands as someone's else,

The color of fading color, lastness
Pluralized because going to sleep

Keeps redoing the translation
Without fully having done. But this

Only applies to *Beim Schlafengehen*
From the *Four Last Songs* of Strauss.

D'HAUSSONVILLE
(FROM *PEOPLE ON SUNDAY*)

A town no one lives in
Must be everywhere around us
Accounting for the hysteria
Of any pose. As we see into
The laugh of things fields or folds
Of wrinkled blue appear divided
Into secondary propositions
Of a primary fact, that fronts are lighter
Than backs because attention glows
And the body offered for inspection
Tries to master this overlit house
By pointing up specific parts,
One hand at the neck pulse while
The other wraps or reprises the waist.
None of which should be visible
In the mirror behind but is, nor should
Flowers grow up out of the dark
Of the back but they do, for centuries
Now without getting any larger.
It doesn't help that the right arm around
Her waist seems to grow from her torso
Rather than her underwhelming shoulder
Or that the left arm's elbow drives
Up from resting on the right hand,
Intent on ending in a hand of its own,
Which surrounds and supports the canted chin
Only by indicating it exists in space.

I happen to know for a non-fact
It was raining on this particular day
So no reason to have the face
Display any obvious flowers
Of an agony collected everywhere
Beyond the frame in Haussonville,
Where it only rains outside,
Where Ingres set off the entre-nous
As a repopulated network of the glance
Figured also in the interior monologue
The surface of her body causes. You
Can see the modern prison forming too
If you close her eyes, which are and are not
Looking at you, a glance with two fronts,
Two backs, a front and a back, or a half.
"That's where she lacks support" (overheard
On the 51B at College and Alcatraz)
But I trust support is there, a past
Of intentional oil spills across canvas.
It was flowering out that endless day,
Writing down a copy of the red,
Pink, yellow, and white of other
Days, each the only example
At hand. And no matter who you are
She is bemused and pessimistic
Your damage can see her padded hurt
Though by her I mean the hand of Ingres
To which both of hers invisibly point
Throughout. This is happening and not
Happening, like the things in a mirror
Whose frame escapes the picture's own
And has a candelabra attached to it
But no candle, not even an unlit one,
So daylight and the phantom presence
Of a forgetful servant who could have been
Called by the blue bellrope closely

Tracking down that part of the mirror's gilt
Frame the painting allows us to see.
What else do we ever know but that
Torsos sitting on hips the way pots
Cut flowers have been dropped in rest
On credenzas themselves covered in blue velvet
Are what is only partially occluded here.
It's been done before; even admitting
It's been done before's been done, but not
In Haussonville, where it rains supports
Of all kinds, and variations on blue,
Enough to populate a sitting room
The single figure richly parses,
Trapped in what has been called
A rainbow of blues, deep but narrow
Luxury reflected in a mirror
Into which you can and can't possibly be seeing
Accurately. She would go on to write
Romantic novels and historical studies
Without her left hand ever leaving
Her chin, the chin of a great-granddaughter
Of Louis XVI's finance minister, Necker,
The last Comptroller General of Finances
Of the Ancien Regime. It is 1842
But is this Paris or Haussonville? Yes,
But there's more, because she is further
The granddaughter of Mme. De Staël
So that all this trivial importance stacks
Behind her glowing face like the eighty
Studies Ingres made for the portrait,
Including sixty for the gown alone,
While the many blues of the painting
Pass into and out of the uniform shade
The revolutionary army's soldiers wore,
Now reduced to the "storm of approval"
With which the painting was received

By friends and family. She also wrote
A biography of Byron, which her gown
Has already begun in its pleats.
Like the dream of seeing hidden things
And the hugest processes therein
The blue only refers, is "of," genetic
And hard to kill off. It is 1845
Forever when the painting is completed
Though she herself is no longer
Twenty-four or anatomically
Incorrect as he has made her here.

QUICK TRIP
(FROM *EXPERIENCE IN GROUPS*)

It was just a time of matter, that zone
Between running and stopping
Bred of gas and twilight
Where all speech is eloquent
As the outlines of cars and stores.
Always just twilight, hence speech
Always eloquent, caught between
Massing and dispersal. There people
Possess the eloquence of eloquence
While we watching have our uselessness.
I hear fall will come, but not for any of us.
I hear it will be here, but not as we
Would have it, a burning tire,
Driverless rains that seem commanded
Because of such economy as is.
All scenes are hunting scenes.
There's no good way to be, we must
Not say so. Nothing to do
But kick yourself down the service road,
A forgotten lane, flat on the ground
Or against a brick wall, slammed there
Temporarily, rights draining
Like a crowd gone quiet, so it is said.
Poetry would have you believe that
Words are acronyms while the state
That acronyms are words. You can't
Yet be rescued from this earth.

So the suburbs politely burn
And the ringroad, the QTs.
It will happen again means
Dark blue can't be outrun,
A verdict known before it comes.
I hear of it from as far as my lap.

EXPERIENCE IN GROUPS
(FROM *EXPERIENCE IN GROUPS*)

What is language is a new needed
For the going on part of the end
You can tell has made it here because

The air is with condition
The outside seems to be like anything
Placed in a lab or subway car

The truths are showing through
The people have chosen to be
Each moves along fresh tracks

On the erasable surface
Toward a tiny destiny
Wearing in and out

It's maybe three days after
Or exactly during seeing
The future put on those certainties

I want of the opposite to speak
To say what isn't etymology, won't
Be money to the king above my eye

Reach out to the invisible third
Among every two pedestrians
Where belonging bucks its norms

And difference can live in least places
Shine caught in the multiple
Lie of any kind of hair

You can't tell if it's order or not
To follow the too many paths
Just above the face, below sky

Long enough to forget or be
Distracted from the big geographies
Where truth first learned of us

In the pit of an education
In the skysick life of power
In its moving rearrangements

I was walking on Mission Street
In love with you while damage bloomed
The right order right in the words

Below the preserved fade of marquees
The little sale of needless things
Listing bodies syntaxed past

It was far too easy to get here
Standing still while white time flowed
Around its professional mourners

Comfortable in end after end
The next one isn't very pretty
At least we'll see how together

It provides absent alternatives
My plan to put my body between
Where it already was and is going

SIMPSON FAMILY LITERARY PROJECT
WRITING WORKSHOPS

SIMPSON FELLOWS
&
WORKSHOP SELECTIONS

AN UNBEARABLE TENSION:
ON JAMES BALDWIN
AND THE NATION OF ISLAM

BY ISMAIL MUHAMMAD

SIMPSON FELLOW

CONTRA COSTA COUNTY JUVENILE DETENTION;
MT. MCKINLEY HIGH SCHOOL;
CONTRA COSTA COUNTY LIBRARY
MARTINEZ, CALIFORNIA

One night in the fall of 2003, during my first semester in high school, I reclined in bed and read James Baldwin's *The Fire Next Time* in one sitting. An LAPD helicopter made endless revolutions above my neighborhood as I cradled the book in my hands and turned its pages—gingerly, lest the reverie I'd fallen into evaporate just as suddenly as it had descended upon me.

I was a fourteen, perhaps the same age as Baldwin's nephew James, and I thought that in writing to James he was writing to me as well. When, in "My Dungeon Shook," Baldwin asserted that the "black man has functioned in the white man's world as a fixed star, as an immovable pillar" whose decision to move might shake society to its core, he'd conferred upon me an identity I'd never known before. I was not a black boy in a white world, condemned to interminable and internecine conflict with white America, but a black boy whose status as a human being afforded me an agency and dignity that could not be pried from me. To encounter Baldwin was to encounter myself floating free, unhinged from the axis around which I'd been rotating my whole life.

My enthusiasm thinned upon reading the volume's second essay. Whereas the "My Dungeon Shook" is an affirmation of black people's ability—their duty, even—to fashion an identity separate from the *nigger* fantasy of white America's imagination, "Down at the Cross" is a sober and incisive indictment of American race relations, and a call to accomplish a destiny that, fifty-four years removed from the book's publication, seems elusive as ever. We find Baldwin wrestling with the new contours of the "Negro Problem," the dangers of which multiply exponentially in the wake of the Holocaust's unfathomable violence. For him, Nazi Germany's genocidal campaign against European Jews excavates new depths to the white supremacist order's murderous disdain for people of color. These depths are enabled not just by technological process, but also by the indifference and savagery white supremacy engenders in the human heart. The possibility that such violence might erupt in America—and that black people will be its inevitable targets—haunts Baldwin.

"For my part, the fate of the Jews, and the world's indifference to it, frightened me very much," he writes. "I could not but feel … that this human indifference, concerning which I knew so much already, would be my portion on the day that the United States decided to murder its Negroes systematically instead of little by little and catch-as-catch can." But Baldwin's fears aren't confined to what white America's hatred of black people might manifest. He's also concerned with the reaction the Holocaust might trigger in African American minds. Confronted by the stark revelation of the barbarity at the Western's world's heart, how will black people respond? Will they undertake the thankless task of love that the white man himself cannot bear to shoulder, or will they turn to unvarnished hate? For Baldwin, the fate of the democratic experiment seems to rest on this question.

He finds a disturbing possibility in the Nation of Islam, a black separatist organization that joins aspects of Black Nationalist ideology and Islamic theology. Founded in Detroit in 1930 by Wallace Fard Muhammad, the Nation teaches that African Americans aren't American at all, but God's chosen people, members of a lost Islamic tribe stolen from Africa and stranded in the West. Fard, who materialized in the city during the tail end of the Great Migration, prophesied that God would deliver them from their earthly suffering and destroy their white oppressors, who weren't humans at all, but devils in disguise. In this new world, African Americans would have their own nation, carved out of the Southern states. Fard Muhammad's converts thought him to be the messiah, arrived to usher in a new social order. Though he vanished in 1934, the organization continued expanding for a time under the leadership of Elijah Muhammad and Malcolm X.

Fard Muhammad built his organization by proselytizing to Southern refugees—recently arrived in Detroit–who escaped the Jim Crow South's rigid caste system and routinized violence, only to contend with Northern segregation. For so long, they'd choked on a bitter ideology that told them they were subhuman and unworthy of respect. They must have been ravenous for something heartier, for anything that told them they were possessed of dignity and explained their miserable place in American society.

For Baldwin, this dream is a pernicious lie, nothing more or less than white supremacy's mirror image. He considers them twin ideologies that rest on the same principle: "the glorification of one race and the consequent debasement of another." The Nation merely inverts America's racial hierarchy rather than upending it, replacing the Christian West's white God with a black one. Standing on a crowded Harlem street corner, Baldwin hears a Nation minister speak and concludes that, "as theology goes, it was no more indigestible than the more familiar brand asserting that there is a curse on the sons of Ham … it has been designed for the same purpose; namely, the sanctification of power."

In short, the Nation represents Baldwin's worst fear come to life: that African Americans, rather than eschewing white supremacy's poisonous racial politics, might embrace it as the basis for a new but no less unjust social order, one that is not worthy of the pluralist promise embedded in American democracy's principles.

An unbearable tension seized me upon reading Baldwin's critique of the Nation. Though his insistence on love—not a feeble thing to be granted easily, but a tough-minded understanding that insists on accountability for America's wrongs—moved me, I also possessed a perspective that Baldwin dismissed out of hand as naïve and morally bankrupt.

I grew up in Los Angeles as a member of the Nation of Islam.

◆◆◆

As a child, I swallowed the Nation's ideology as easily as the Harlem residents Baldwin observed, though my life couldn't have been further from their suffering. My mother and father escaped poverty and used their resources to provide my brother and I every material advantage denied to them as children.

But trauma's reach is long, and a mere change in economic fortune can't ease its grip. Despite my parents' success, they had come of age during the racial ferment of the 1960s and '70s. They had witnessed too much of America's reaction against racial equity for the Civil Rights Movement's faith in democratic progress to imprint itself on them. They were not yet teenagers when Martin Luther King Jr., was assassinated, and their sense of America's racial politics took shape in the aftermath of the Watts and Detroit riots, and subsequent white flight from the inner cities. In an era when a paroxysm of brutal violence presaged America's retreat from its responsibilities, my parents found the Nation of Islam's explanation of racial politics as plausible as any other.

The glossy optimism of Bill Clinton's America wasn't the dominant tenor of my childhood. I came of age in the shadow of Ronald Reagan's racial counterrevolution, and my parents taught me how white supremacy continued to damage black communities. I didn't have to harken back to the Jim Crow past to understand this. In the 90s, South Los Angeles— then a majority black region suffering from de facto segregation and an economic collapse—resembled a tomb filled with the walking dead. Spurred on by widespread joblessness and a failing education system, gang activity had become a fixture of our reality, and few families weren't touched by the violence that plagued our streets. Meanwhile, the crack cocaine epidemic's lingering effects were plain to see in damaged eyes of every relative who'd fallen prey to the drug. Every challenge assailing my community confirmed that the white world was engaged in a conspiracy against black life. I knew few white people, but white supremacy's fruit was plain to anyone who had eyes. It was nothing to me to think that the absent people who inflicted such damage were devils. I was young, but already my parents' fear and anger had become my own.

Baldwin doesn't dismiss the anger and bitterness that such conditions generate. Reflecting on the hatred that settled into his childhood church congregation, he concludes that, "the Negro's experience of the white world cannot possibly create in him any respect for the standards by which the white world claims to live." For him, the Nation of Islam's explanation for inequity is predictable human reaction to living under oppressive conditions. Baldwin doesn't want to dismiss that anger—he is, after all, concerned with humanizing African Americans, imbuing them with the psychology and emotional life that the *nigger* figure banishes—but he certainly can't condone an ideology that sanctifies prejudice.

Ultimately, though, he is unable to treat the Nation with the soft insight he brings to reflections on his childhood church. Early in "Down at the Cross," he seems to condemn his congregation for embracing Christ as "a measure of how deeply we feared and distrusted and…hated almost all strangers, always, and avoided and despised ourselves." In the very next paragraph, though, Baldwin relents, admitting, "But I cannot leave it at that." After all, he has *lived* in this congregation, and he knows it as a living community whose bitterness belies a nuanced set of rituals that bind individuals together in a complex humanity.

Baldwin is not so charitable to the Nation. He reserves no such mercy for its members because, ultimately, he has not lived their lives. There is something of a limit to his seemingly boundless empathy. When, in the essay, Baldwin looks at a Nation of Islam member, the writer can only perceive the young man as an unwitting, vacuous fool who is "held together, in short, by a dream."

I wondered what Baldwin would see if he looked at me. What if he dared to look harder?

◆◆◆

In the nineties Los Angeles sky was still laden with smog, and while it was terrible to breath it turned the city's sky into a spectacle. So at dawn I awoke not just to pray, but also to admire sunrises that were riots of pink and orange light streaking across the sky, and linger at my window to admire the sight of multi-colored clouds slowly moving across the sky like globs of oil rising to water's surface. As my parents taught me, I'd perform my morning ablutions before dawn, sweep the living room floor, and fall into silence as I waited for the sun to rise. Then I'd make *salat*. I'd memorized the prayer so well that its words tumbled from my mouth without any particular effort: *In the name of Allah, the beneficent, the merciful...* Meanwhile my mother would enact a curious ritual: my mornings began with gospel music's tones rousing me into the day, so that often the first thing I'd hear was either Aretha Franklin or Mahalia Jackson's voice slinking through the house, preparing the day before my feet hit the floor.

My mother, the daughter of a Southern migrant, grew up as a Christian in a Baptist household, and I don't think she's ever considered the Christian ritual she borrowed from her youth to be at odds with the Islamic ritual she'd adopted in her adulthood. Singing along to Aretha's version of "Mary Don't You Weep," she'd improvise, replacing "Jesus" with "Allah" with an agility and ease belying the fact that she was melding two disparate cultures. For my part, I grew up thinking that black Christianity and Islam were complementary, so much so that I saw no problem in letting my grandmother, who lived with us, read to me from the Bible, or even in attending her Baptist church from time to time. My family mingled and switched between various cultural practices with the ease with which a bilingual person alternates between languages.

This was the household in which I was raised, a point of intersection where myriad cultures converged and cross-pollinated one another. Though the Nation of Islam's rigid doctrine of racial separation informed my earliest conception of race relations, my lived experience—which wouldn't have been possible outside of the Nation's bounds—taught me that cultural and racial identities are malleable, that they exist on a continuum where cultural elements interpenetrate one another to form an intricate mesh.

In this sense, the Nation is a strange chimera, a peculiarly American amalgam that's always demonstrating the fitful fulfillment of what Ralph Ellison called "the mystery of American cultural identity": the protean nature of a nation whose culture is premised on incessant and chaotic exchange.

This is the nuance that, for all of his empathy and understanding, Baldwin can't quite capture. It's something that I implicitly understood when, in 2000, my parents enrolled me at Orville Wright middle school, an impressively integrated public school on the city's Westside. There, I was assigned to honors courses where most of the other faces were non-black ones. I had my first intimate contacts with students of other races—including white kids, whom I only knew through a representation as outlandishly distorted as Baldwin's *nigger*.

But it's difficult to doubt someone's humanity when they stand before you in the flesh. I ate with these children on the blacktop, exchanged mixtapes with them, spent afternoons at their houses playing video games, and met their families. This newfound familiarity was not always easy – sometimes these people's behavior left me bitter and confused, as when they touched my hair without my consent, or lost interest in me when I failed to meet their expectations of how a black kid should behave. But even these incidents were lessons to teach myself how to be black in a multiracial space. Interracial community was no longer inconceivable; it had become something concrete, a site for recurrent dialogues that helped build understanding and empathy. This was a community that my friends and I had to achieve as best we could, not one that we could lazily slide into.

Discovering Baldwin codified and confirmed my experience. *The Fire Next Time* was proof that someone had trod this ground before me, and had vouchsafed not just for the possibility, but the *necessity* of the community I was building. I took Baldwin's condemnation of the Nation to mean that my freedom was not merely a matter of *power*, as Fard Muhammad had preached, but also of an exit from morally bankrupt racial politics that white supremacy had initiated.

As I've aged, though, I've also been struck by how much Baldwin could not see, by all the places his empathy could not go. If I ultimately outgrew my life in the Nation of Islam, it is because the Nation unwittingly provided me the tools to do so. My childhood faith was more a part of the American pluralist promise than Baldwin could have known.

UNTITLED

BY J. P.

How could I sleep
While stuck in a cell?
Close my eyes shut
All I picture is hell.

Thoughts in my head making me think,
I'd rather be dreaming of counting sheep.
Crossing days off my calendar
Wishing it was a dream.

Thinking of my family
How they doing without me.
I'll finally go to sleep
When I awaken from this bad
Dream.

UNTITLED

BY I. O.

I keep my helmet and cleats
You can tell I'm in the field
Playing with my faith.

Don't really mind if I lose,
Lost a couple games already.
Got me thinking 'bout my next move.

Should I sit on the bench or score?
Don't know what to do, Lord
Please help me make my next move.

I'm stuck in the field,
My teammates keep falling.
The other team is not playing fair.

I want to talk to the ref,
But he's not there.

PHOENIX

BY S. R.

Born from hate and disgrace
The stain of rejection dyed my clouds gray
The heat of the sun engulfed me

The love and passion binds me
Got me wrapped up
In the past of misery

Thinking of the family I don't deserve
The mornings I walk in the kitchen
The crisp smell of cooked bacon

This family gave me the love that I seek
I'm blessed with the time I got to have with them
I don't have to keep all this pain tucked away

I recall all the love that I have received
That gives me the courage to rise above
By walking a path of a family man

I must rise to the challenge and come up a victor
By taking chances of responsibility
Born in the light of bravery

CITYSCAPES IN MATING SEASON

BY LISE GASTON

SIMPSON FELLOW
NORTHGATE HIGH SCHOOL
WALNUT CREEK, CALIFORNIA

Car alarm bird calls blast the dusk. Seagulls wheelie the burnt sky. Crickets stridulate their four types of cricket song, parading the cement field under the Atwater overpass. The city thrums with it, ready to blow. Summer calling. Night fogs windows with its warm breath. Fingers unbend from the blurry dark to trace crooked hearts on every pane. Like you, night has a lovely mouth.

Death in his black dress plugs the parking
meter at the end of my street. He'll stay as long
as he damn well likes, but he still has to pay for
it. His huge black engine idles—squirrels
throw themselves at its moaning flame. The
engine runs its tongue over their small bodies,
under their skin. Little skulls pop beneath tires
on the road. Death counts his change to the
penny: he likes the new ones, how they shine.

Was it that moment of my mouth over yours, drawing our breath out? In my apartment we engage in wonderful destruction while below us the girl with the red dress and violent lips walks down my street and angels spark from her eight-cylinder rib cage, holy and obscene, rending red cloth in the warm night. The maples, ablaze, haul up their roots and scatter panic through the city like foxes with tails on fire...

At Parc Laurier, in the rain, dogs lick quartz from stones, lick their owners with glittering tongues. Under the clouds, silence coagulates, catches in air vents and storm drains and screeches choking through the metro. It takes my breath away, this ground. And in the park, I see Buddha's head on a stump, areolar pouches of blood dripping down his neck, the whole head red like blood and gleaming in the thick wet air.

A dame walks into a bar on the corner, all tall on the ruin of her long legs. The sidewalk drools on itself, giggles and retches with civilized scents of terrier shit and apricot beer, the sweetness of deep-fried meat and salt and—the ocean, the ocean I miss its smell, its muscular, furred tongue. The dame stumbles home. Guilt curdles in the bar walls, then one night burns the dark place down.

The city is full of beautiful boys—in doorways, on bicycles, long hair swept from delicate faces. But I keep finding the empty shape of you, over my shoulder, lined in earth-rot under cedar boughs. Your body stretches in the spaces between cars waiting for the light. You've drunk half my beer you bastard, I know it. Otherwise, whose lip marks there, whose thumbprint on this frame?

SIMPSON WRITING WORKSHOP
STUDENT WRITING

NORTHGATE HIGH SCHOOL
WALNUT CREEK, CALIFORNIA

LISE GASTON, SIMPSON FELLOW

SUNSET IN MEXICO

BY ELIANA GOLDSTEIN

A taste of sea salt
In the humid summer air, which cools
By the time the orange sun sets
Rests on my silent pink tongue
That runs across my dry,
Full lips.

As night draws nearer, and the sun
Drifts closer to the edge of the green
Blooming mountains,
The horizon darkens and waves
Grow closer to the eighteen-story
Hotel on the shore.

A hurried and trying day ends
In a peaceful evening of turning frayed, yellowing
Pages that smell like libraries
And men's scented candles,
Listening to the sounds of crashing
Waves and singing seabirds.

Children run across
Tiny grains of beige
Sand, soft under new, playful
Feet, innocent and free spirited
Minds and bodies, dancing their way
Across ocean ground.

There's an arbor not far from
The ocean's edge, flowered and empty,
Waiting. A slanted path, carpeted
in brilliant grass, leads to
The arch, welcoming
Flowered brides and their fathers.

I can almost see myself
Tracing that path in my snow-laced
Gown, violins singing and bells sounding,
Someone waiting
Under the red wooden arbor,
Dressed like a prince,

Smiling like a princess.
Their eyes meet mine,
Glistening
In the setting sun's light,
The light just fading
From the heavens.

A smile tugs at the side
Of their lip, and we are blessed with
An eternity together,

with a single, blissful kiss.

WINTER

BY ELIANA GOLDSTEIN

Cold,

It feels true and strong, though
It's only an illusion
Simulated by an absence
Of the warmth I crave.

The biting teeth tear
Apart my skin
Scattering freckles
As my shell fades
Into a state of numbness
Expanding and then disappearing.

It's too cold for
The clouds to cry;
It would harden into ice.
It's possible for there to be
Just maybe
A lighter, dancing, flourishing ice
But not here.
It will not snow, though

I wish.

CALEF AVENUE

BY GRACE DECKER

From the outside, the house doesn't seem like much. The paint is chipped in most places and even though you can tell someone clearly planted flowers in the yard, the grass is overgrown and it's all muddy in the back. But in the end, none of these things matter. What matters is standing on the third floor balcony listening to the sound of the ocean, squinting to try and see it in the night even though it's only a hundred feet away. It's the sound of muffled voices from upstairs, and being afraid to go up to the third floor at night because it's always so dark. It's finding new places to explore every day, and feeling like everything is just at your fingertips without even leaving the house. It's running around in the back and realizing that this is what having roots feels like. It's missing something you are too young to even understand, and not realizing that everything is changing around you. But what matters the most in the end of it all is touching the side of the house as you leave for the last time without knowing it'll be the last time, and driving away without looking back.

A LAZY MIDSUMMER BRUNCH

BY LOGAN VENDEL

Time and space are not exactly as you think. There is no straight progression or fixed structure, not even an interconnected blob. The entire universe as we know it is really a picnic. All of space and time, sprawled out on an endless green countryside under a cloudless blue sky, compressed into the fixings of a lazy midsummer brunch.

The fabric of reality is a checked blanket with everything nestled in it, under the shade of an ancient oak. Stars and planets, dust and people. Perhaps the cheese is a galaxy, the wine a nebula, bread and jam and meats glittering and swirling with the brilliant majesty of a billion stars. The centerpiece, however, is something even more strikingly beautiful.

It is a cake, coated in frostings of blue and green, of brown and white, the colors of the splendid earth. The cake on its shining black pedestal is the centerpiece, and as the celestial beings sit and eat, sipping stardust, their twinkling eyes are drawn to its magnificence. As they grow full one of them will pick up a vast cake knife spotted with the light of some far-away star, and dig deep into the earth, gouging a slice out and passing it to one of the other picnickers.

They pass these slices around and as they eat things get jumbled. The layers of this cake are time, split and forked into eager mouths. As they chew, those great beings feel time, they feel the passage of the aeons, the chocolate layer the Mesozoic period perhaps, a raisin or a cherry the impact of a meteor or some upheaval of tectonic activity.

Humanity is only a garnish atop the vast sea of time, but as the layers are mixed the human race is scattered through it all. Kings and peasants ride the backs of immense beasts, trampling through primitive seas. Hunters and farmers and poets and soldiers scramble through a rich jungle, wading through lava and mud and pure, clear streams. With all that came simpler sights and sounds and smells, mountains rising and falling, seas growing and shrinking, plants and animals living and dying and evolving.

Brimstone and sulfur and morning dew. Cliffs worn away in the blink of an eye, only to rise back up from the sea, volcanoes and earthquakes and storms and floods, thousands and millions of them, catastrophe after catastrophe, but always a lingering calm.

The full human experience merely a subtle aftertaste, a strange sweetness and bitterness full of blood and music and triumph and failure, barely noticed but strangely savored.

The picnickers ate and grew full and lay onto the backdrop of the universe, and they looked into the blue sky and marveled at its beauty.

TRAVELING

BY LOGAN VENDEL

Nary a tarry for a traveler or two,
Wandering from town to town under a moon of blue.
Never a moment to sit down—
We're only passing through.

REFUGEE

BY JACKSON MILLS

The train pulled into King's Cross station, and a thousand souls departed at once. With the masses came a little boy, his face expressionless, entering a world unknown to anyone on that train. He began to cry on the station platform. Hardly anyone noticed, as hordes of people made their way to the exit, the foreign world still above them. But the boy remained, crying and slightly slumped over, as the breeze from the departing train whisked up a few leaves. Then a woman appeared from the adjacent lift and knelt beside him. "What's wrong, little boy?" she asked. The slight smile on her face briefly calmed the boy as he turned to look at her. Then he began to cry again.

"What am I going to do without my family?" he stammered between sobs. "I miss my mom, my dad, my sister. I can't live in this new world; I miss my town, I miss my home, I miss my family! How can I live here with nothing? I know nothing! I've lost everything on the journey to leave a life not worth living, but life is still not worth living here."

The woman did nothing but gaze at the little boy's tearful, unkempt face for several long, painful seconds. Her concerned, uptight expression did not change. Crowds of people walked briskly by. Another train pulled into the station, the passengers regular commuters as usual. More tears streamed down the face of the boy.

Then the woman took the little boy's hand; and smiled. "Come," she said. "This world is so lucky to have you. Let's make sure you feel lucky living in it."

They walked to the escalator leading to the world above them. The woman did not notice right away, but the little boy had stopped crying by the time the escalator reached the surface.

NOT MY MAMA

BY LIVIA DOPORTO

Mama used to tell me pretty was the most important thing. "You can go to school but it won't do a damn thing," she'd slur while she knocked back her fourth beer, "It's the pretty girls who move up in the world. They marry the smart boys." I told her I wanted to be a lawyer one day. "Ha!" she laughed in my face, "you're never getting out of this town. You'll be sixteen and pregnant just like the rest of us." Then she'd walk away, laughing down the hall.

When I was thirteen an older girl won an internship in Chicago. She was a talented writer, at the top of her class, scholarships lined up for when she graduated. She never made it though. She got pregnant and stayed in Missouri with a baby she couldn't afford and a drunk for a husband.

At fourteen I signed up for the spelling bee. I put on my best dress, combed my hair, and snuck out my window to catch the bus. Mama wouldn't have wanted me to join the spelling bee. I won against every kid in our county that day, about 150. My winning word was intelligible. I-N-T-E-L-L-I-G-I-B-L-E. I ran home with my trophy that night to show Mama. When I came in she was passed out on the couch. Daddy was watching baseball in the back. I hid the trophy in my closet and lay in bed silently, pretending to be asleep. Mama never knew I won the spelling bee.

When I was fifteen a boy asked me on a date. I had never been asked on a date, but every girl in my grade had a boyfriend already. Mama's words echoed in my head, "sixteen and pregnant just like the rest of us." I had bigger dreams than a boy could smash so I said no. The boy had grown up never hearing that word. Shocked, he pushed me to the ground and kicked me hard in the ribs. I ran home with tears down my face. Mama asked what happened, and I told her I tripped. I had a big bruise on my side and pain for weeks. Mama had the same bruise. She said it was because she tripped too.

At eighteen, I graduated from school. A hundred kids in my class and only twenty-five got their diplomas. I moved out three days after graduating. I told Mama to move with me. "I could go to school and you could get an apartment, find a job in the city somewhere." She didn't answer, walked down the hall and let me leave without saying goodbye. Her life was there, she was pregnant at sixteen, married at seventeen, just like the rest. But I wasn't gonna be my Mama.

JUST A SMILE

BY LIVIA DOPORTO

Sometimes when men smile at me I feel it against my skin.
Like long fingernails dragging across my arms
All the way up to my bony shoulder blades
Down through my chest
       Then a tightening deep in my stomach
The feeling drags all the way down through my toes
Until the eyes upon my body are released from my skin
But the feeling remains etched into my heart
       Each look digs a deeper hole in me, telling me to be cautious
Telling me that it is my fault I am looked at and my fault I am scared.
And each time I am stared at I shrink a little smaller
Until I am become nothing but fear of eyes of a man
A man I've been told to beware of
       But has anyone told this man to stop his stare?

POEMS

GIRLS INC.
OAKLAND, CALIFORNIA

LAURA RITLAND, SIMPSON FELLOW

GARDEN LEAVE

Ingrown affection for the garden. An intention,
drawn from the shed drawer, cuts through
the rose-heads. The scene needs reordering:

a life's work is what it's called. Through the past's
undergrowth, my arm carves a new relation
to the sun: an event for which the outcome

is its use and a good reason to appear busy on a weekday.
It only looks like repetition. What I love is difficult
and knows no appropriate end—the architecture

confuses. The overshot branch springs out of hand.
Forget the form for a season, it shifts
after rain. The mind's an unreliable workman

when it comes to judging difference. Uproot
the incomprehensible and you leave off understanding.
Let the shears do the talking. Change serves beauty

better than expectation. As through a green tower
one opens windows. As with time, new faces
return your gaze through the thorns.

INTERVIEW WITH THE BODY

Hands, you did well to respond to the doorknob
although your handshakes lacked the vigor

of a live fish. Legs, you may not walk fashionably
in the lilt of slim nylons, but you conducted us to sit

at the interviewers' panel with routine deliverance.
I am grateful for this even now as we blow-dry

our nerves softly in a public bathroom. While many
have pondered these identical sinks in panic, none

have paused here in this exact temperature of sweat.
Mouth, I forgive you for smudging my future's vowels.

Voice, while you writhed like a snared skunk,
you tried to express us. After all, how to have said

our best work was done standing outside
of ourselves? That, physically, we clank

and the knee's instinct is a miracle? Chest,
you may not remember when you were five

hands painted red hearts over your lungs.
Face, once your mother made you into a tiger.

MARINE ECONOMY

They hear the moon shaking the sky with white noise.
Waves stings their eyes, beads their lashes with salt.
They brace their knees against the sea's robbery, thorny shins

against gravity's knock. Neighbours' thighs pressed in rows
constellate their total galaxy. Stars, they lie petrified
inside brittle houses as sculpins prowl the crusted avenues.

Tides are their presidents. Sea currents minister their economy.
In their chalk city, every element matters exactly
how it occurs. Too little moisture means death. A dry summer bakes

even the toughest heads cracker-dry. Come breeding season,
they hook up either or both of their two gonads, throw their billion
children to the sea in hopes that one might grow old.

Blind, the crawling heart will search the ocean for the flavour
of a new home. A freak gust of water, a rogue current
and all's lost, overboard; these are civilians of chance's law.

But their species knows their own taste like the scent of bread
in the dark. Finding its trace, it pastes a foot next
to itself in the only world it knows to be natural.

**SIMPSON WRITING WORKSHOP
STUDENT WRITING**

GIRLS INC.
OAKLAND, CALIFORNIA

LAURA RITLAND, SIMPSON FELLOW

IT STARTS WITH YOU

BY TIFFANY TONG

Imagine
you wake up
with a second
chance
You hear bombs
drop
destruction widespread
screaming and flailing
as they go
hurt and hungry
inmates on death row
Then
one thing you do
interrupts the flow
There is something
the commander
must know:
These are children of God
of spirit they bore
So now sir,
may we end this Yemen war

HALF OF A HEART

BY KERRY LIN

The heart is an organ that helps us stay alive,
 delivering blood to places in the body to help us thrive
where the veins and arteries intertwine
 with vessels so intricate like twirling vines.
Supposedly, it represents love and our soul,
but our own hearts are only halves,
 and two make a whole.
The color of it is mostly red, some yellow and a little blue
 and eventually
it will stop
when the time is due.

THE DARKNESS

BY MICHAELA DUNAWAY

Imagine you wake up
with a second chance:
the darkness stares at you
like a beautiful rose
slowly wilting
you run from it.

But then
you pause, turning around slowly
only to see the darkness not chasing you.
You begin to look at it
as though there is something in it
or maybe more like someone.

It's just you
in a happier state.
You start to realize that the darkness isn't your enemy.
It's a reflection
of not just you, but the choices you've made.

You welcome the darkness in your arms
like it was your mother
or someone that loved you so much that it hurt
and then everything becomes warm.

You say you don't regret anything
and you don't need a second chance
because you made every day of your life
a second chance.

DEFENSE: A MEMOIR

BY MICHAELA DUNAWAY

Over the course of my life, I have been put into many different activities like hip-hop dancing and acting class. But the one activity that impacted me was Kung Fu.

Although I wasn't excited about it at first, I met a lot of different students there that made me change my mind. My instructor or "shifu," as I was told to call him, wasn't as intimidating as I thought he would be. He was very happy and nice, but he knew when to be tough. The other students, although they were my friends, intimidated me. Their skills were much more structured and powerful, while I felt like I wasn't giving it my all. I wanted to be at their level physically and mentally. I worked hard each class, sometimes forgetting that my purpose there wasn't to be perfect, but in fact know how to defend myself.

I began to earn more belts, but I still felt as if I was lagging behind and still weak. Part of me started looking at my friends in the class with pride while the other side only saw sadness. Sadness of how I still felt like I couldn't accomplish anything. Time away from the class made me reflect on what I could do to make that cynical part of my thoughts go away. I started practicing at home and stretching more.

The next time I went to class happy to see everyone I put more effort into what I was doing to make myself feel stronger. But when I took my exam for my next belt, I felt the intimidation set back in. Everyone who was taking a test in that room was a lot younger than me. In my head, I was hoping that they wouldn't be that good.

They were really good, even better than me. When it was my turn, all the parents and the little kids stared at me. The intimidation and fear started to consume me in a dark hole no matter how hard I tried to fight it.

The only thing I can really remember from that day was me breaking a board with my foot which shifu did not prepare me for. Shockingly, my foot went through the board so easily though when I checked my foot later it was really red. Earning my belt and certificate the next day made me realize that even though my skills weren't as superb as my friends', I was okay with that. I am capable of so much.

I continue to see my actions in life this way. People will always expect something from you based on whether you show it or not, but all that matters is what you are capable of doing. You are the only one who can decide if you are strong and if you don't think you are strong it's because you are not thinking about just you. You are too focused on something or something else judging you. Life is going to be filled with intimidating things and people, but it's up to you to either let it consume you or overcome it.

CONTRIBUTORS

Joseph Di Prisco is Founding Chair of the Simpson Family Literary Project and author of fourteen books of fiction, poetry, memoir, and nonfiction. His most recent books include *Sightlines from the Cheap Seats* (poetry; 2017), *The Pope of Brooklyn* (a memoir; 2017), and *Sibella & Sibella* (a novel; 2018). He grew up in Brooklyn and Berkeley, and now lives in Lafayette, California. He received his PhD from the University of California, Berkeley. He has taught English and creative writing, and has served as Trustee or Chair of several non-profit boards devoted to education, the arts, theater, and children. diprisco.com

Ben Fountain was a finalist for the 2018 Simpson Prize. He was born in Chapel Hill and grew up in the tobacco country of eastern North Carolina. A former practicing attorney, he is the author of *Brief Encounters with Che Guevara*, which won the PEN/Hemingway Award and the Barnes & Noble Discover Award for Fiction, and the novel *Billy Lynn's Long Halftime Walk*, winner of the National Book Critics' Circle Award and a finalist for the National Book Award. *Billy Lynn* was adapted into a feature film directed by three-time Oscar winner Ang Lee, and his work has been translated into over twenty languages. His series of essays published in *The Guardian* on the 2016 US presidential election was subsequently nominated by the editors of *The Guardian* for the Pulitzer Prize in Commentary. His new book is *Beautiful Country Burn Again: Democracy, Rebellion, and Revolution*. He lives in Dallas, Texas with his wife of thirty-two years, Sharon Fountain.

Lise Gaston was a Simpson Fellow (2018). She grew up on both sides of Canada, in Fredericton and Victoria, and has also lived in Toronto, Halifax, Montreal, and Limerick, Ireland. Her poetry, essays, and reviews have appeared in journals across Canada, the United States, and Ireland, including *Arc Poetry Magazine, European Romantic Review, The Fiddlehead, Lemon Hound, The Malahat Review, Matrix Magazine, Numero Cinq,* and *Prairie Fire.* Her writing has won awards in *Arc*'s Poem of the Year and How Poems Work contests, and has been selected for *Best Canadian Poetry in English 2015.* She is a graduate of English and Creative Writing programs at the University of Victoria and Concordia University in Montreal, and is now a PhD Candidate in English at the University of California, Berkeley. She divides her time between Berkeley and Edmonton. *Cityscapes in Mating Season* is her first book.

Samantha Hunt was a finalist for the 2018 Simpson Prize. She is the author of *The Dark Dark: Stories,* and three novels. *Mr. Splitfoot* is a ghost story. *The Invention of Everything Else* is about the life of inventor Nikola Tesla. *The Seas,* Hunt's first novel, will be republished by Tin House Books in 2018. Hunt is the recipient of a 2017 Guggenheim Fellowship, the Bard Fiction Prize, the National Book Foundation's 5 Under 35 Prize and she was a finalist for the Orange Prize. Hunt has been published by *The New Yorker, The New York Times, The Guardian,* and a number of other fine publications. She teaches at Pratt Institute in Brooklyn and lives in upstate New York. samanthahunt.net

T. Geronimo Johnson was the recipient of the 2017 Simpson Prize. He was born in New Orleans. A graduate of the Iowa Writers' Workshop and a former Stegner Fellow at Stanford, Johnson has taught writing at UC Berkeley, Stanford, the Writers' Workshop, the Prague Summer Program, Oregon State University, San Quentin, and elsewhere. He has worked on, at, or in brokerages, kitchens, construction sites, phone rooms, education non-profits, writing centers, summer camps, ladies shoe stores, nightclubs, law firms, offset print shops, and a (pre-2016) political campaign that shall remain unnamed. He also wrote a couple of novels that have—between the two—been selected by the Wall Street Journal Book Club, named a 2013 PEN/Faulkner Award finalist, shortlisted for the 2016 Hurston/Wright Legacy Award, longlisted for the National Book Award, longlisted for the Andrew Carnegie Medal for Excellence in Fiction, a finalist for The Bridge Book Award, a finalist for the Mark Twain American Voice in Literature Award, included on Time Magazine's list of the top ten books of 2015, awarded the Saroyan

International Prize for Writing, and named the winner of the 2015 Ernest J. Gaines Award for Literary Excellence. Johnson was a 2016 National Book Award judge. He lives in Berkeley, CA. geronimo1.com

Anthony Marra was the recipient of the 2018 Simpson Prize. He is the author of *The Tsar of Love and Techno*, a finalist for the National Book Critics Circle Award, and *A Constellation of Vital Phenomena*, longlisted for the National Book Award and winner of the NBCC's John Leonard Prize, the Anisfield-Wolf Book Award, the Barnes and Noble Discover Award, and Greece's Athens Prize for Literature. He has received the Guggenheim Fellowship, the Whiting Award, the National Magazine Award, the Berlin Prize Fellowship, and his work has been translated into seventeen languages. In 2017, *Granta* included Marra on its decennial Best Young American Novelists list. He has taught at Stanford University, and currently lives in Oakland, CA. anthonymarra.net

Ismail Muhammad was a Simpson Fellow (2018). He is a writer and critic based in Oakland, California He's a staff writer at *The Millions*, a contributing editor at *ZYZZYVA*, a board member at the National Books Critics Circle, and a PhD candidate in the English department at UC Berkeley. In addition, he's been a recipient of the National Book Critics Circle Emerging Critics Fellowship and a participant in the VONA 2017 workshops. His work, which focuses on literature, art, identity, and black popular and visual culture, has appeared in publications like *Slate, New Republic, Los Angeles Review of Books, Real Life,* and *Catapult.* He's currently working on a novel about the Great Migration and queer archives of black history. ismail-muhammad.com

Joyce Carol Oates is Joyce Carol Oates. She is also the Roger S. Berlind Distinguished Professor of the Humanities at Princeton University, and a member of the Simpson Family Literary Project Committee. She is a recipient of the National Book Critics Circle Ivan Sandrof Lifetime Achievement Award, the National Book Award, and the PEN/Malamud Award for Excellence in Short Fiction, and has been nominated for the Pulitzer Prize. Her books include *We Were the Mulvaneys; Blonde*, which was nominated for the National Book Award; and the *New York Times* bestseller *The Falls*, which won the 2005 Prix Femina. She has been a member of the American Academy of Arts and Letters since 1978. In 2003 she received the Commonwealth Award for Distinguished Service in Literature, and in 2006 she received the Chicago Tribune Lifetime Achievement Award. Her work of non-fiction on grief and bereavement, *A Widow's Story*, was a critically-acclaimed success. Her most recent novel is *Hazards of Time Travel*.

Geoffrey O'Brien is Professor of English at the University of California, Berkeley, and a member of the Simpson Family Literary Project Committee. He was educated at Harvard University and the University of Iowa. He is the author of several poetry collections, including *Experience in Groups* (2018), *People on Sunday* (2013), *Metropole* (2011), *Green and Gray* (2007), and *The Guns and Flags Project* (2002). His work is part of *Three Poets: Ashbery, Donnelly, O'Brien* (2012), and he collaborated with poet Jeff Clark on *2A* (2006). He also teaches at San Quentin State Prison.

Lori Ostlund was a finalist for the 2017 Simpson Prize. She is the author of *After the Parade* (Scribner, 2015), which was shortlisted for the Center for Fiction First Novel Prize, and was a Ferro-Grumley Award finalist and a Barnes and Noble Discover Great New Writers pick. Her first book, a story collection entitled *The Bigness of the World* (UGA Press, 2009; reissued by Scribner, 2016), won the 2008 Flannery O'Connor Award, the Edmund White Debut Fiction Award, and the 2009 California Book Award for First Fiction. Stories from it appeared in the *Best American Short Stories* and the *PEN/O. Henry Prize Stories*. Lori has received a Rona Jaffe Foundation Award and a fellowship to the Bread Loaf Writers' Conference. She is a teacher and lives in San Francisco with her wife and cats, though she spent her formative years in Minnesota, cat-less. loriostlund.com

Martin Pousson was a finalist for the 2018 Simpson Prize. He was born and raised in Acadiana, the Cajun bayou land of Louisiana. *Black Sheep Boy*, his novel-in-stories, won the PEN Center USA Fiction Award and a National Endowment for the Arts Fellowship, and it was featured on NPR's *The Reading Life*, as a *Los Angeles Times* Literary Pick, and as a *Book Riot* Must-Read Indie Press Book. *No Place, Louisiana*, his first novel, was a finalist for the John Gardner Fiction Book Award, and

Sugar, his book of poems, was a finalist for the Lambda Literary Award in Gay Poetry. He is a Professor in the College of Humanities, California State University, Northridge, where he teaches in the Creative Writing Program and the Queer Studies Program. martinpousson.com

Laura Ritland was a Simpson Fellow (2018). She is a PhD student in English at the University of California, Berkeley, and the author of *East and West*, a book of poetry. Her poems have appeared in *The Fiddlehead, CNQ, The Walrus, Maisonneuve, Arc Poetry Magazine*, and *The Malahat Review*. A recipient of the 2014 Malahat Far Horizons Award for Poetry, she currently divides her time between Vancouver and California.

Scott Saul is Professor of English at the University of California, Berkeley, and Emeritus Simpson Family Literary Project Committee member. He is a historian and critic who has written for *The New York Times, Harper's Magazine, The Nation, Bookforum*, and other publications. The author of *Becoming Richard Pryor* and *Freedom Is, Freedom Ain't: Jazz and the Making of the Sixties*, he is also the creator of "Richard Pryor's Peoria"—becomingrichardpryor.com—a digital companion to his Pryor biography that brings to life Pryor's formative years in Peoria's red light district. He teaches courses in American literature and history and lives in Berkeley, California, with his wife and son.

Simpson Family
Literary Project

simpsonliteraryproject.org